Criticism and Social Change

Frank Lentricchia

Criticism and Social Change

The University of Chicago Press

Chicago and London

FRANK LENTRICCHIA is Autrey Professor of Humanities at Rice University and
Director of the Program in Humanities. He is the author of *After the New Criticism*,
Robert Frost: A Bibliography (with Melissa Lentricchia), *Robert Frost: Modern Poetics
and the Landscapes of Self*, and *The Gaiety of Language*, a study of Yeats and Stevens.

The University of Chicago Press, Chicago 60637
The University of Chicago Press, Ltd., London

©1983 by The University of Chicago
All rights reserved. Published 1983
Printed in the United States of America

90 89 88 87 86 85 84 83   54321

Library of Congress Cataloging in Publication Data

Lentricchia, Frank.
  Criticism and social change.

  1. Criticism.   2. Literature and society.   I. Title.
PN81.L42   1984   801'.95   83-9299
ISBN 0-226-47199-3

For Bernard Duffey

"e tu maestro"

The one thing in the world,
of value, is the active soul.
—Emerson, "The American Scholar"

You can't *see* the class struggle.
It is an *interpretation* of events.
—Kenneth Burke, *Attitudes Toward History*

There is nothing that does not need to be
studied in class, including, of course, the
oddity of studying in a class. Everything
and everybody, the more randomly
selected the better, has to be subjected to
questions, especially dumb questions,
and to the elicitation of answers. The
point is that nothing must be taken for
other than "strange," nothing must be
left alone. . . . And if in fact some things
cannot be taught, then that in itself
should be the subject of inquiry.
—Richard Poirier, *The Performing Self*

Acknowledgments

A number of my friends, in whom intelligence and generosity reside in rare unity, read parts or all of the manuscript: Michael Harper, Tom Haskell, Paul Jay, Wes Morris, Richard Poirier, and Carolyn Porter. David Miller made a number of suggestions that helped me to improve the fourth part of the book. Hayden White triggered the entire project when he asked me to contribute to his and Margaret Brose's volume, *Representing Kenneth Burke*. I am grateful to Hayden for that, but even more for his immense gifts of friendship and support. In his customary elegant style, Perry Anderson gave me a tough critique and a strong boost when I needed both. It was Myron Simon who led me to the speech that Burke gave at the American Writers' Congress; though he couldn't have known it at the time, Myron was leading me to my most searching reconception of my project. *Grazia*.

Parts of this book were read at Santa Cruz, CalTech, Claremont, Irvine, the English Institute, the University of Vermont, Emory, the University of Alabama, Rice, George Mason, the Bryn Mawr/Temple "Conference on the Philosophy of the Human Studies," Columbia, and Carleton College. Each of those public occasions gave me the opportunity to rethink my style and argument, and to all those who extended me invitations to lecture, I am grateful. I want especially to thank Tom Vogler of Santa Cruz for inviting me to test my ideas, then in embryonic stage, in a three-week seminar for graduate students. Though they didn't know it when they asked me to lecture at the Theory of Literature seminar at Columbia, Edward Said and Marie-Rose Logan pushed me through some late but important rethinking.

I must mention my indebtedness to Amy Lentricchia, now twelve, for delivering in a recent letter to me a stinging critique of a friend's materialism (of the nonhistorical sort). And I am continually grateful to Rachel Lentricchia, now ten and a half, for enlightening me with frequent Joycean puns—her most recent a commentary on my attitude toward history: "hystery."

In the words of the immortal O. C. Smith, Melissa Lentricchia "keeps on keepin' on." If you know O. C. Smith, or Melissa and her work, you will know exactly what that means.

The debt that I—really all of us—owe Kenneth Burke is incalculable. I hope that what I have written honors what he stands for.

This book is for Bernard Duffey who showed and shows me what an intellectual can be. He was and is my teacher.

Provocations

I can tell you what my book is about, at its polemical core, by citing a distinction of John Dewey's that I first encountered in the amazing meditative labyrinth Kenneth Burke called *Attitudes Toward History*. The distinction is between "education as a function of society" and "society as a function of education."[1] In the end, that is a way of dividing the world between those who like it and those who do not. If you are at home in society, you will accept it, and you will want education to perform the function of preparing the minds of the young and the not-so-young to maintain society's principles and directives. Such a relationship between society and its educational institutions Burke calls "normal," and what he intends by this is roughly the irony that Michel Foucault extracts from the term—education will involve itself in a process of "normalization," of *making normal*, of ensuring that its pedagogical subjects will be trained (taken through the human equivalent of the process of dressage) so that they will be happy, useful, productive, and safe subjects, in the social and political sense of the term: they will be cunningly "subjected."[2] With the proper transformations accounted for, we might say that being a "normal citizen" is akin, in Thomas Kuhn's scheme for scientific community, to being a "normal scientist." If you hold such a theory of education, you are a conservative. Insofar as you think the order should be reversed, that society should be a function of education, you are a radical or that strange, impossible utopian, the radical in reverse gear we call a reactionary. (To complete the picture: liberals, in this scheme, are nervous conservatives governed by an irresistible impulse to tinker, though when the chips are down, they usually find a way to resist their need to mess with the machine.) The radical of either the progressive or the nostalgic type is not at home in society; the radical feels alienated and dispossessed. As Burke puts it: "To say that 'soci-

1

ety' should be a function of 'education' is to say, in effect, that the
principles and directives of the prevailing society are radically
askew (that the society has been despoiled of its reasonableness)
and that education must serve to remake it accordingly."³

Now, if the social project of the reactionary can't be taken
seriously on its own terms, and if liberalism is mainly an illusion,
we are left with two political choices: conservatism or radicalism—a convenient opposition of terms which needs some complicating. Of the two, conservatism always has the massive sustaining power of inertia on its side. The difficult project of the
radical is to break that force somehow, and one of the questions I
will pursue is whether a "break" is possible, in the strict sense,
and if not, to what degree the radical act is thereby compromised,
made itself conservative. Is the historicity of action a block, a real
subversion, or is it the favorite excuse of the self-conscious university intellectual to do nothing and to sink into occupational
nihilism? To what degree is an act possible that would not be
wholly and by necessity an act of sustaining and conserving? Can
the radical "remake it"? Can a literary intellectual, to come to the
issue that most preoccupies me, do radical work *as* a literary
intellectual?

I come down on the side of those who believe that our society
is mainly unreasonable and that education should be one of the
places where we can get involved in the process of transforming
it. So stated, my position gives me no comfort at all, since what I
have called the reverse radical holds the same position (Jerry
Falwell thinks it unreasonable, too). My position will eventually
need a lot less pragmatism, but before it needs less, it will need
more. To return to Dewey: his notion that society should be a
function of education is not nostalgic, for it bears no reverence for
the past. The (mostly unarticulated) social theory of pragmatism
tends to stem from a view of mind—that the "pursuance of future
ends . . . [is] the mark and criterion of the presence of mentality in
a phenomenon"—and its corollary that the object of knowledge
is not some completed entity, temporally antecedent, and therefore impervious to human action: the object of knowledge for a
pragmatist is "possibility" itself, in a strict sense a nonobject
whose being or nonbeing will depend upon our action and especially upon our ability to establish a satisfactory relation with it.⁴ It
is not hard to see some of the social and political implications of

the pragmatist theory of knowledge: all brute social givens, all customs, all authorities in place—these and the powers that sustain them—do not fare too well. Pragmatism, then, is the quintessential American point of view, the philosophical rationalization for a new adventure for history and culture founded on the rejection of the Old World and all of its encrusted precapitalist evils. Only an American pragmatist could have written the following, which is at once a political critique of classical, spectator epistemology and an alternative to it: "The real object is so fixed in its regal aloofness that it is a king to any beholding mind that may gaze upon it."[5] Pragmatism is a rejection of hierarchical structure itself, of the stabilizing (kingly) forces of structure, which would always stand safely outside structure—outside the game, but ruling the game. Pragmatism is a commitment to the openness of time and a chance for change; pragmatism, then, is the expression of the radical democrat and the experimental method, or scientific spirit of democracy. But is pragmatism also the authorization of a ruthless individualism? A rationalization of the robber barons and the business ethic? Do these embarrassing questions point to an abuse of pragmatism or to one of its inherent tendencies? Think of the archetypal narrative of the capitalist, say, Flem Snopes from the literary world or Andrew Carnegie from the real one, and you will have two luminous examples of what it might mean to say that proof of mind in a phenomenon is its pursuance of future ends, or that pragmatism is a commitment to the openness of time.

Pragmatism at its critical best may underwrite the radical democrat and a healthy distrust of authorities, customs, entrenched prejudices, and repressive structures which pass for common sense. But the scientific side of pragmatism—its desire to control and plan our relations to our social and natural environments—history has proved to be problematic, to say the least; and its underwriting of the self-centered capitalist spirit of rugged individualism is more than troublesome. The undecidability of pragmatism's social position comes from the stance it takes on behalf of the lone existential individual and against the collective, the Big Organization. In Dewey this undecidability shows up in his inability to put together a mainly Jamesian epistemology with the historicist and even socialist cast of some of his late books of social theory. In *Liberalism and Social Action*

(1935), scientific inquiry becomes, as it had for C. S. Peirce, the very image of social cooperation and community, the figurative contrary of the rugged and ruthless capitalist. Nevertheless, pragmatism's feeling for the individual is so strong, its animus for *a priorism* so powerful—this is especially clear in William James—that it stretches the concept to the breaking point to say that pragmatism has a "social position." Given James's hatred of the collective, we might even conclude that pragmatism should take a stance against the social.[6] So when a pragmatist urges that society should be the function of education, we have to ask what kind of society do you want education to produce? The real pragmatist may have to contradict himself in order to answer the question, because to be a pragmatist is in a sense to have no theory—and having a position requires having a theory. The liberating, critical move of pragmatism against the "antecedent" is compromised by its inability—built into the position of pragmatism as such—to say clearly what it wants for the future. Though not practice for its own sake, pragmatism cannot say what practice should be aimed at without ceasing to be pragmatism, without violating its reverence for experimental method. It cannot specify the imperative without falling back into the rationalism that it so categorically hates. Pragmatism's best insight, that knowledge is an instrument for doing work in this world, cannot help us to do the social work of transformation implied by the Deweyan slogan "society as a function of education."

There is another, even more self-subversive element at play in pragmatism's social intention. By poising "society" and "education" against each other, undialectically, the pragmatist implies that education can stand in pure opposition to society, directing its critique and would-be transformation from somewhere "outside" the social space of its scrutiny, "free" from the contaminating things it would change. Society, in this view, is a function of education, but education would be a sort of *ding an sich*, an unsituated function of nothing at all. Pragmatism's mostly uncritical celebration of the uncontextualized individual is another expression of a deeply ingrained tradition of antinomian American individualism, which returns here to haunt pragmatism's nascent social theory. Heavily committed in its theory of knowledge to the openness of the temporal process, to the futurity of knowledge, and to the knower as isolate antinomian experimenter, pragmatism drains from its epistemology all but a minimal residue of history and society. Located outside all sociohistorical space in existential time, the cognitive subject in pragmatism cannot draw upon existing social practice for an alternative critical sociality, the new society that it would generate in its educational function. This rigorously undialectical level of pragmatism would seem, if pressed hard enough, to demand a dialectical integration: society can be a function of education only if education is also a function of society; the practice of a critical pedagogy must emerge from, be irritated into existence by, its own discomforting social ground.

Probably to no one's surprise I'll set pragmatism aside (though not out of sight) for Marxism, which had already included pragmatism's key insight about the instrumentality of ideas and theories but had placed that insight within a fully elaborated vision of history and society. Ideas not only have material effects; they have material circumstances as well. Historical materialism, unlike pragmatism, says that ideas can have material effects only because they have material circumstances. Knowledge is the production of classes, institutions, and disciplines, and the mode of production itself, not of isolated individuals. "Production of"—the grammatical ambiguity (genitive or possessive?) will have to stand: its resolution in one direction would take us into the idealistic *a priorism* of "Young Hegelianism"; in another, into the mere materialism of the base/superstructure model. The airy ineffectuality of idealistic *a priorism* has been savagely detailed in *The German Ideology* and numerous other texts in the orthodox Marxist tradition; the latent totalitarianism of the base/superstructure model, though a less celebrated focus of Marxist self-analysis, has been explored and, to my mind, convincingly demonstrated in Herbert Marcuse's early work: ideas which merely reflect practice or are after the fact apologies for it but cannot critically guide it, become unreflective things in themselves; like the essences of phenomenology, they simply are, they are not to be questioned. This is a Stalinist position. If intellectuals will put themselves in that position they will save totalitarians from having to do the brutal work of intellectual repression.[7]

This is a book that leans on some insights of the Frankfurt school (Max Horkheimer's distinction between "critical" and "traditional" theory is important to me) and also on insights of the pragmatist and rhetorical traditions which are at best only a marginal part of Marxism's strong orthodox history. In a limited sense this is a "Marxist" book; in many senses, it is unrecognizably Marxist. For American intellectuals, pro and contra Marx, this is probably as it should be. While it may be close to impossible to think about progressive change without engaging Marxist categories, one of the lessons to be drawn from Kenneth Burke's career is that an American ("self-reliant") Marxism is fundamentally an absurd proposition. The "active" critical soul in America, from Emerson to Burke, joins parties of one, because it is there, in America, that critical power flourishes.

In its most general intention, this book is about culture, intellectuals, the authority and power of intellectuals—how intellectuals, in their work in and on culture, involve themselves inescapably in the political work of social change and social conservation. More particularly, this is a book about the literary intellectual—but those two words, most of all, need comment. By *literary intellectual* I mean the sort of intellectual who works mainly on texts and produces texts: hence not only poets, novelists, and other "creative" writers and literary critics in the narrow sense but all intellectuals traditionally designated as humanists; critics in the broadest sense; and not only university humanists, but also literary intellectuals in the sense of journalists, advertising experts, and all media creators and disseminators of what is called "the news": people who read, analyze, and produce what advanced criticism calls "representations" and "interpretations." My focus is the university humanist, because I think that his and her position as a social and political actor has been cynically underrated and ignored by the right, left, and center. By "intellectual" I do not mean what traditional Marxism has generally meant—a bearer of the universal, the political conscience of us all. Nor do I mean a "radical intellectual" in the narrowest of understandings of Antonio Gramsci—an intellectual whose practice is overtly, daily aligned with and empirically involved in the working class. By intellectual I refer to the *specific intellectual* described by Foucault—one whose radical work of transformation, whose fight against repression is carried on at the specific institutional site where he finds himself and on the terms of his own expertise, on the terms inherent to his own functioning as an intellectual.[8] The university humanist may organize teach-ins about the situation in El Salvador or in Beirut; he may work for the improvement of conditions for what we in the university call "staff" as opposed to faculty; he may involve himself publicly in political work in the so-called outside world—he may do all of these things, and these are all genuine and important political acts, but these acts often have no necessary relationship whatsoever to his or her specific, detailed, everyday functioning as a teacher of, let us say, expository writing or American fiction, and as a writer in those fields. My presiding contention is that our potentially most powerful political work as university humanists must be carried out in what we do, what we are trained for. We might do it very well because we have the technical knowledge of the insider. We have at our disposal an intimate understanding of the expressive mechanisms of culture. We know how culture works; we know, or should know, that culture does *do* work. I would go so far as to say that those of us in the university who conceive of our political work mainly in those other ways I have listed, and not as activity intrinsic, specific to our intellectuality (our work as medieval historians, for example) are being crushed by feelings of guilt and occupational alienation. We have let our beliefs and our discourse be invaded by the eviscerating notion that politics is something that somehow goes on somewhere else, in the "outside" world, as the saying goes, and that the work of culture that goes on "inside" the university is somehow apolitical—and that this is a good thing. We have sold ourselves on our powerlessness because first of all we have sold ourselves—our traditional training has sold us—a deceptive idea of the relations among culture, society, and power. To believe as university humanists that our political work can only be in the streets, or in the factories, or at best in writing essays and books about Reagan, Vietnam, or the Middle East is to leave traditional cultural power to those forces that wish to engender in us the feeling that we are ineffectual angels. That inside/outside distinction is killing us.

This "we" that I refer to, this radical literary intellectual is at the same time (here we must turn the screw on Gramsci's conception of the intellectual) "traditional" by his educational confirmation even if his social origins are working class. And though in some significant sense his struggle must be against himself, against his own training and history as an intellectual, and against the culture that he has been disciplined to preserve, his very traditional personal history as an intellectual, if critically appropriated, will turn out to be one of the real sources of his radical cultural power. So except in a few rare instances, the radical literary intellectual in American universities will emerge out of and be indebted to his former traditional self. Against that very generalization, and on behalf of the rare instance, I would say that the intellectual of working class background, or more broadly of a background outside the social, racial, ethnic, economic, gender-biased, and homophobic mainstream, will in effect have to retrieve his outsider's experience, bring it to bear in critical dialogue with the traditional confirmation he has been given.

I need to complicate this matter with a personal example that a number of American intellectuals with my sort of background may share. This kind of intellectual, who has been confirmed "traditionally" in the educational process and who more and more is becoming a presence in American universities, will need to retrieve his outsider's experience; but having done that, he will find that his desire for radical social action—assuming that he feels such desire—will have to work through the mediation and the manipulation of the peasant origins of his immigrant (in my case, Southern Italian) grandparents. Going back to your roots in a simple way is no answer. Like the lives of his grandparents, he will find that his life—his desire—has been marked (appropriated) by a distinctly feudal social formation; his life as an intellectual will tend to represent not an organic elaboration of an exploited group—its political vanguard—but a gentrified escape from and repression of his social and ethnic sources. My son the university teacher will not be screwed as we were; like a *padrone*, he works only six hours a week. To become an intellectual from this kind of background means typically to try to forget where you've come from; it means to become a traditional intellectual in Gramsci's strict sense—a cosmopolitan gentleman of the world of letters, philosophy, and art. "Making it" in my kind of context, then, may be one of the most insidious forms of betrayal, because the conditions of "success" underwrite the social and political interests of that *padrone* who exploited our ancestors.

To our delight—we've proven that we're as good as they are—we of the third generation win jobs in the professions, as only the sons of the *padrone* could in the old country. The exploitation of the first generation, however, rarely receives its critique because, for complicated reasons, no or very little critical memory in its sons and daughters actively survives, or is encouraged or educated—not even at home. The social structure that exploits immigrant workers (and all other workers) is reinforced by the attractive model for success and freedom, for a really new life, which America offered to those who came to its shores from abroad. If we third generation Italian-Americans can make it (so it goes), so can the sons and daughters of America's Black and Chicano ghettoes. This is not, after all, the old country—here we all have the chance. If you don't make it, says the myth, then you are lazy, or you just weren't lucky enough to be born with brains. In any case, whatever our social background, our struggle as critical intellectuals will be inescapably as much with ourselves as with the culture and society we would oppose because "they," in a sense, are "us."

The would-be specific literary intellectual who wants to work for social change will, in addition, have to fight off two demons of self-doubt: one from the orthodox left, who will tell him that his work is bullshit and that real political work lies in the organization of workers; the other from the ultra left who will tell him that he must connect his work on traditional texts directly to the "real" situation, our contemporary political situation, directly to the front-page news, or risk total apolitical rarefication. My answer to these demons is that genuine political work for the Henry James scholar, as Henry James scholar, becomes possible when contact is made with the activity of James's writing, with all possible emphasis on its *act*. I believe that nothing less than that answer risks accepting not only the irrelevance of the literary intellectual but also the most reactionary reading of Marx that I know: the unhistorical materialist reading (mere mechanical materialism) that reduces to irrelevance the work of the mind by telling us that "History" (now with a capital letter) will eventually make everything come out O.K. One who calls himself or herself a Marxist must be sensitive to the charge of anti-intellectualism, for within Marxism anti-intellectualism carries a terrible political burden. In an essay on the politics of interpretation, Edward Said, echoing a question put by Terry Eagleton to Fredric Jameson, asks how a Marxist reading of a minor novel by Balzac can "shake the foundations of capitalism."[9] He answers, of course, that it won't. Is it necessary to say to Said and Eagleton (who are both sympathetic to Jameson) that no single individual act—certainly no single intellectual act—will shake the foundations of capitalism? The question that Said and Eagleton raise projects the sardonic, irritated tone of engaged intellectuals who have seen reams of ineffectual prose pumped out by their humanist colleagues. The irritation is understandable, but in this case it is not only misdirected: it lurches toward despair of the useful work that might be done in the academy, and maybe even toward personal disintegration. The difficult truth that Said and Eagleton know above most others (but it's easy to forget in our exhausted academies) is that struggles for hegemony are sometimes fought out in (certainly relayed through) colleges and universities; fought undramatically, yard for yard, and sometimes over minor texts of Balzac: no epic heroes, no epic acts.

"The philosophers have only *interpreted* the world, in various ways; the point is to *change* it."[10] A Marxist literary criticism—and I insist again on the broadest sense of "criticism" and "literary"—would need to start there, with the eleventh of the theses on Feuerbach: the point is not only to interpret texts, but in so interpreting them, change our society. Theories of reading or interpretation (theories are interpretations of interpretation) help us to do intellectual work, but even to say it that way, to speak of *intellectual* work, courts an idealism, a split between theory and practice that is the secret ground of despair for most academic intellectuals. And I am not sure that Marx's eleventh thesis on Feuerbach entirely escapes such debilitating idealism. Marx's point is that philosophical interpretations more often than not produce no social change; what they do produce, he suggests, is a *gnosis* disengaged from radical *praxis*. Unfortunately the apparently indifferent interpretation of the philosophers is not, despite Marx's implication, apolitical; in the strict sense it is politically conservative. For praxis only in some circles implies radical intention; in most circles social effect is not synonymous with social change. Interpretation that shores up things as they are or prevents social change by encouraging resistance to it, by encouraging the view that change is illusion—because action itself, which would produce change, is too problematically beset by unavoidable historical repetition; or interpretation according to traditional humanism that routinely separates culture and power—these sorts of interpretation produce powerful social effect. For certain kinds of social philosophy and criticism, such interpretations, such "disinterested" ways of reading and teaching, are indispensable modes of action. Interpretation always makes a difference; the philosophers always do something more when, and as, they interpret the world.

Criticism, I am arguing, is the production of knowledge to the ends of power and, maybe, of social change. This kind of theory of interpretation presupposes a critical theory of society and history—what human beings have made, they can and will unmake and then remake and remake again. But if we have learned anything from what is called deconstruction in France and the United States, it is that the context of one's literary readings (in my case a critical theory of society and history) is itself an interpretation. If the one thing in the world of value, as Emerson once said, is the active soul,[11] then the kind of activity that a Marxist literary intellectual preeminently engages in--should engage in—is the activity of interpretation, an activity which does not passively "see," as Burke puts it, but constructs a point of view in its engagement with textual events, and in so constructing produces an image of history as social struggle, of, say, class struggle, an image that is not "there" in a simple sense but is the discovery of the active intellectual soul.[12] This sort of interpretation, when worked through the traditional texts of the humanities, will above all else attempt to displace traditional interpretations which cover up the political work of culture. An active, self-conscious work of interpretation will show the political work that the canonized "great books" have done and continue to do. Gramsci's definition of critical consciousness (the act of knowing yourself as the product of a historical process that has deposited its traces in you) will stand, with some extension, for the definition of a critical consciousness of texts: the act of "knowing" the text as a product of struggle, a way of "interrogating" the text so as to reproduce it as a social text in the teeth of the usual critical lyricism that would deny the social text power and social specificity in the name of "literature." The activist intellectual needs a theory of reading that will instigate a culturally suspicious, trouble-making readership. Whether or not one calls oneself a Marxist, one could, I'd say one should, always check one's effectivity as a teacher of the literary classics by asking oneself the following questions: Does one's approach to the text enable or disenable—encourage or discourage—oneself and one's students and readers to spot, confront, and work against the political horrors of one's time? Does our week-in and week-out work in the classroom open our eyes, or does it not? Do we feel at all times, *as* teachers and *as* writers, involved in the real thing, or are we continually choking down suspicions that what we do, and where we are, is not in the real world? If our conceptions of literature politically disarm us, then so much the worse for our conceptions of literature.

So what is the status of Marxist literary theory? In orthodox Marxism, this question eventually gets bogged down in metaphysics, generally entailing a teleological idea of history (the ultimate context for all traditional Marxist acts of interpretation) and an epistemological claim that Marxist discourse on the historical process has a privileged epistemic status, since a Marxist discourse can adequately represent the foundations of historical process, the real drift of things. I do not take the view that Marxism has that sort of claim upon us; I do not believe that Marxism or any other philosophy rests on the foundations of reality or history. In the old sense of the word, Marxism is not a "true" theory. With Richard Rorty, I am ready to set aside the classical claim of philosophy for representational adequacy. In its place, I am ready to urge (Rorty is not) a materialist view that theory does its representing with a purpose. This sort of theory seeks not to find the foundation and the conditions of truth but to exercise power for the purpose of social change. It says there is no such thing as eternally "true" theory. It says that theories are generated only in history—no theory comes from outside—for the purpose of generating more history in a certain way: generating the history we want. The claims I am making against "true" theories are not themselves grounded on some ultimate "true" theory of purely historical nature. My historical claims make no traditional epistemological demand on my reader; they are points of departure for the work I do. Because I conceive of theory as a type of rhetoric whose persuasive force will not be augmented in our time by metaphysical appeals to the laws of history, the kind of Marxist theory that I am urging is itself a kind of rhetoric whose value may be measured by its persuasive means and by its ultimate goal: the formation of genuine community. Marxism as a kind of rhetoric, a reading of the past and present, invites us to shape a certain future: an invitation to practice, not epistemology. The main work of Marxism, as I see it, following Gramsci, is hegemonic: the establishment of consent, of a "we." History, then, is a kind of conversation—but not in Rorty's sense—whose discourse is rhetorical and without foundation and whose ends are never assured because rhetorical process, unlike teleological process, is free. It assumes that people do things not because they must but because they are persuaded to do them. Marx without science: rhetorically laced discussion, not violent coercion, with the ends of the conversation up for grabs—Marx without Stalin.

Although I've ruled out for myself the classic Marxist appeal to teleological drift—a nineteenth century metaphysical Marxism, which we cannot make believe is not an important theme in the corpus of Marx and Marxists—at this point I have to say that I cannot resist the limited historical claim to truth in Marx's reading of capitalist society, in the limited historical context within which he carried it out. His analysis of the structure of commodity capitalism and the class system and culture it spawns and undergirds, though it fails at some crucial points for our context, yet continues to exert a compelling pressure upon us, and it does so because his context is in some deep sense ours. Marx does not offer his reading as a misinterpretation or a fiction, even though the "truth" of his reading and the praxis he links to it are grounded in purely historical reason and are necessarily for *that* reason always subject to revision. His respondents, those on his side and those not, in effect grant their contextual continuity with Marx and the persuasive power of his analysis. Reagan can and in effect does agree with the less contentious descriptions of capital within Marxism when he speaks on behalf of "free enterprise," but he would not agree that such description implies the sort of evaluation and subsequent action that Marx's language at every point implores. Again, is Marx's picture "true"? Does it "correspond" to social reality? The answer is that, through an analysis of existing conditions, an analysis penetrated by an astonishingly powerful vision and rhetoric, Marx created a picture which Marxist and many non-Marxist intellectuals today in the West respond to as if it were true, as if in fact this is where we live, what our history at bottom is all about. Marx's picture, in other words, is true not in the reflectionist terms in which it is often posed (and which dialectical theory must reject) but in the pragmatist sense that it has put many intellectuals into active and rich commerce with their society. It is a necessary though not sufficient context for all thought of social action. It is precisely at that point, when we take Marx out of science and insert him into the politically combative zone of culture that this book begins. Because it is precisely at that point that Marx's analysis becomes a contestant, along with other contestants, in the war of ideas which will help to decide the social shape of things for us—what our lives will have to bear. As cultural weapon to be deployed in social struggle, Marxist theory is a form of will to power, because what I am calling "culture" is knowledge precisely at the point at which knowledge becomes power, or is on the way to power.

Is there culture that is not covert politics? I can conceive of cultural effects apparently not political, but such effects seem to me to be of little interest. I can conceive of cultural effects which are rigorously aesthetic, but the history of aesthetics, which is a secret argument over the fate of sensuousness, is a thoroughly political history of the containment and defusion of sensuousness in what the Germans called *Schein*. "Culture," in this text, is intertwined with "power"—and the history of the word, as Raymond Williams tells it, especially in its earlier usages, is worth recapitulating. "Culture" is derived from the Latin *Colere*, meaning, among other things, *to inhabit*; in an early English form, it refers, as a noun of agricultural process, to an activity of tending—*the tending of*. Then this leap in Milton, which picks up *inhabit* and *tending*: "Spread much more Knowledg and Civility, yea, Religion, through all parts of the Land, by communicating the natural heat of Government and Culture more distributively to all extreme parts, which now lie num and neglected."[13] *Inhabit, tend, spread*, until the numb and the neglected are no longer so—are one of us. In these politically active senses, culture becomes a validation of the state, a process whose goal is saturation of the social—a point made vigorously by Edward Said.[14] A criticism for social change, while it must understand the intention of cultural domination, can take its place as a criticism situated within resistance only if a space of resistance is left open, only if a dominant "culture" cannot completely cover the social. I would say that a criticism on behalf of social change can successfully occupy a space of resistance, however, only if social difference, a primordial given in Marx's theory of history, is not reified—only if social difference can be actively at work within consciousness, regardless of class location. If the inescapable power relation is constituted by the difference of social forces, then critical resistance must be located within that difference or nowhere at all.

Oppositional criticism does not come from outside; it is a necessary effect of the primary power relation that constitutes all social difference in capitalist and Stalinist society. Oppositional criticism is therefore always an active possibility within capitalist society because ruling ideas—situated as they are in a ruling class and distributed from that site through other sites in the society—are nonetheless not situated everywhere, not distributed from every social site. They are not the only ideas. Ruling culture does not define the whole of culture, though it tries to, and it is the task of the oppositional critic to re-read culture so as to amplify and strategically position the marginalized voices of the ruled, exploited, oppressed, and excluded. Cultural domination, or hegemony, as Raymond Williams reminds us, is not a static, finished thing. It is a process that "has continually to be renewed, recreated, defended, and modified" because it is continually being "resisted, limited, altered, challenged by pressures not at all its own." This is to say that hegemony is "never either total or exclusive" and that it is best understood dramatically—I mean agonistically: "alternative political and cultural emphases, and the many forms of opposition and struggle, are important not only in themselves," as Williams puts it, "but as indicative features of what the hegemonic process in practice had to work to control."[15]

I have mentioned Richard Rorty and the metaphor of conversation, and since what I urge intersects his position, might even be taken as a variant of what he urges, let me make some distinctions between my position and what I take to be his. I am in sympathy with his effort to set the classical tradition in philosophy aside, to change the subject, as he puts it. The "conversation" of "culture" cannot be grounded on some natural standpoint called "reality." It cannot be guided and underwritten for the ages by an enterprise that presumes to be beyond culture and history. But because we give up the fiction of a natural standpoint, we will not, in our unconstrained cultural freedom, therefore be released into creativity, strangeness, and other heady breaks through what Rorty (after Dewey) calls the "crust of convention."[16] If we throw the mirror of nature away, we will send the conversation off into new directions, Rorty believes, but because there is no universally commensurate vocabulary we can do no more, he thinks, than generate myriad new directions.[17] No single anchoring goal for the conversation is possible because our various vocabularies will never project or describe the same thing. The voices will tend to merge in a cacophony, a Babel-like chorus of unconstrained and incommensurate interpretations.

Rorty's conversation sounds like no conversation at all. To give up the constraining ground of a natural standpoint means for Rorty to be left with a kind of nominalism of cultural dancers, each moving to the beat of his own drum. We approach Rorty's pragmatist matrix and the antinomian voice that it celebrates. Despite the fact that he comes squarely down on the side of history, against all versions of a "beyond," the problem, here, as before, with the fathers of American pragmatism, is that there is only a rarefied, liberal idea of society or history at work in Rorty's position. The choices for him are stark: either his version of a multi-voiced, uncoordinated cultural conversation or a repressive "reality" that demands a single discourse and a single voice. The missing term in Rorty's analysis is "society," and I suspect that this very absence accounts more than a little for the warm reception his neo-pragmatism has won in American post-structuralist circles.

If we put "society" back into Rorty's analysis, we will quickly see that the conversation is not and has never been as free as he might wish; that the conversation of culture has been involved as a moving force in the inauguration, maintenance, and perpetuation of society; that the conversation of culture, in other words, displays some stubbornly persistent patterns. Cultural action is a shaping power, but it is not original: it is underwritten by something else. You cannot jump into this conversation and do what you please. It is hard to get into; harder still to speak on your own once you do get in; tougher yet to move the conversation in any particular direction that you might desire. For this conversation has been propelled and constrained mainly by collective voices, sociohistorical subjects, not by private ones, not by "autonomous" intellectuals. The involvement of cultural conversation in the social has always borne purpose, but the rhetoric is generally masked and the telos (the exercising—channeling, influencing, distributing, imposing—of a form of social power) is generally invisible. As with the pragmatist move toward the future, so in Rorty we have an attempt to liberate cultural discourses from a past of epistemological repression. He argues persuasively for liberating culture from "reality," but in the absence of "society" from his analysis, and in the admitted reactive, goal-less character of what he calls "edifying philosophy," which he opposes to systematic philosophy (the search for Truth, or at least its conditions), he has difficulty telling us why anyone should want, that is *need*, to be edified. Perhaps the needs satisfied by the pleasures of Rorty's cultural conversation are the liberal, personal needs which literary culture has celebrated from Addison and Wordsworth to deconstruction. The value terms of that literary culture, or variants thereof, we can find at every instance in which Rorty attempts to communicate the reasons why we should engage in what he calls conversation. The words common to Rorty and the literary culture are "strange," "creative," "rare," "original," "different," "new," and "uncanny."[18] These words in the literary culture and in Rorty's writing presumably have no social point, but in fact they do. These are the words used by those in flight from the "normalizing" society that has banished the values which these words stand for. The concluding pages of *Philosophy and the Mirror of Nature* will please those who need a quasi-political rationalization for private intellectual pleasures, but not those who think that culture has something to do with the formation and perpetuation of human societies.

I am not charging Rorty with mere aesthetic decadence, for his is that special critical aestheticism formed in reaction to the repressive specter of a culture that must toe the line of a natural standpoint, in reaction to the societies that have been shaped. Edifying philosophy, like Romantic poetry, would help us to become new beings through its power of making strange. Rorty can believe *that*, however, only if he first believes that our old social being is at the root unsatisfying. Edifying philosophy, down deep, has a goal—it must be both critical and utopian. So in order to be fair to Rorty I will have to admit that the terms "society" and "community" do make a certain kind of appearance in his writing. Their appearance is curiously truncated, however, since these terms refer in the main to potential collectives of human subjects whose integration is wholly grounded in feeling, not in the economic and political dimensions of human activity.[19] When he says that "social hope"[20] must be ungrounded, I think I understand and agree with him. But I doubt that the absence of a traditional epistemological grounding can be replaced by a purely affective one. His key value terms are hedonic; they refer to the possible pleasures of autonomous subjects—maybe that is why he says that "bourgeois capitalist society" is the "best polity actualized so far."[21] The pleasures of imagination, of creativity and originality, are the poetic pleasures of a private subject; it is not clear that they require community. Late capitalist economy, at any rate, seems to be in the business of generating the commodity no longer for its use and exchange values (as classical Marxism would have it) but mainly (as Guy Debord has argued) for its imagistic and spectacular value. Its purpose is to appropriate Romantic literary values such as Rorty's for its own economic perpetuation. One sort of Marxist response to Rorty would be that his values of ungrounded cultural conversation have been decisively co-opted by late capitalist economy. It, too, wants to send things in new directions without reaching any goals, since the classic goals of the commodity are no longer of the essence for the proper maintenance of the economic structure: the Romantic yearning for the new is now transformed into an energetic consumerism.

The literary culture to which Rorty subscribes is out of step with its times: such a culture (for Wordsworth) once possessed critical power because it was directed at an economy devoted to the normalizing sort of production required by emerging big industrial capitalism. In that context, the literary culture's emphasis on the new and on feeling was a healthy effort to rescue us from a gray abstract conformity, the murderous dissection of mass production and the faceless, commodified producers created by such a mode of production. But if the utopian impulse of that literary culture has been pretty much taken over by late capitalism, it has not been totally taken over. Rorty in his social moments speaks, however infrequently, not only of the "exotic specimen" as being one of us—but also of "human solidarity," the need to achieve " 'working harmony among diverse desires.' "[22] These latter Deweyan impulses, as opposed to his

severe Jamesian antinomian impulses, however inchoately
formed, point toward another sort of utopian thrust in Rorty's
work—a community of feelings, of pleasures shared and binding: a fully socialized Romanticism. Such a community is
grounded not in truth eternal, but in agreement of one sort or
another. But to imply that agreement that binds community can
have only hedonic sources seems to me overly restrictive and
maybe dangerous, since the hedonic in itself, fully given into, as
a mode of satisfaction, tends to cut out other kinds of satisfac-
tions, especially those which might be found in efforts at political
intervention. Rorty's vision of cuture is the leisured vision of
liberalism: the free pursuit of personal growth anchored in material security, as John Dewey, one of his philosophical favorites,
suggests.[23] I do not wish to speak on behalf of the Platonic censor
of the mimetic tribe, but only to indicate that the critical rhetoric
which isolates the aesthetic from our political and social lives has
run its course. To say that cultural conversations should be concerned only with what Rorty says they should be concerned with
seems to me to go against the grain of a communal existence. His
interest in human solidarity is attractive, but his edifying mode as
a thinker, by which culture is divorced from political power, can't
make much of a contribution to achieving it. Academically located intellectual communities of deconstructors, edifying philosophers, Anglo-American types, "hard" scientists, and so on,
bear a utopian impulse; they will be actively proleptic, if they are
real communities, for the society we want.

In this book I have attempted to set forth and elaborate a
number of key concepts which I take to be required tools for the
literary intellectual who would be a social force, who at his
specific institutional site would begin to make a contribution to
the formation of a community different from the one we live in:
"society" as the function of many things, one of them being
"education." Not all social power is literary power, but all literary
power is social power—that is probably my central assumption.
The literary act is a social act. My cast is extremely small. Its main
actors are Kenneth Burke and Paul de Man. Burke throughout is
my point of departure, the repository of principles without which
what I think of as healthy criticism cannot function. De Man is
often, in the pages ahead, Burke's antagonist, a repository of
principles which, taken to the place he takes them, promotes a

debilitated criticism whose main effect is political paralysis. These are not, however, allegorical portraits of critical good and evil. Burke I have not always found congenial; in the later sections of this book, I find de Man useful for a politically effective literary intellectual. Burke and de Man are not, then, the binary alternatives of contemporary critical practice, but their difference, as opposed to their opposition, is strong, so strong and influential that it makes a difference for our practice. If the choice to be made is not either/or, it is still a choice, and at some point it must be and always is made. But this book is not about Kenneth Burke and Paul de Man. It is about my work, what I do, and what I would do as a literary intellectual. Like Foucault, I do not believe that what I do has global implications; the social struggle that I often refer to is not exclusively economic and class rooted, although I think it is mainly that. Foucault makes it very difficult for us, in any case, to generalize all struggle and repression as an economic principle. But why should anyone care, finally, about locating *the* source of human misery? There is enough misery for all of us to confront in many different places, in many different forms, much of it not obviously economic. Finding a single source, if there is one, won't make those miseries go away any faster. The point is to work where we are without at the same time regretting that those who struggle elsewhere may never hear our voice.

Part One

I want to begin my pursuit of the issue of criticism as social force with a look at an event in the life of Kenneth Burke, the publication of which in his books and collections he has to this point deferred; an event which, according to his testimony, produced hallucinations of "excrement . . . dripping from my tongue," of his name being shouted as a "kind of charge" against him, a "dirty word"—"Burke!"[1] I am referring to a brief paper Burke delivered to the first American Writers' Congress, held at Madison Square Garden in late April of 1935, organized and attended by the most engaged literary figures in the United States, and featuring a number of distinguished European guest speakers. The purpose of this first congress was to extend the reach of the John Reed Clubs by providing the basis for a much broader organization of American writers. The capitalist system was crumbling rapidly—that seemed undeniable. If writers could effectively band together, then maybe they could accelerate what had to happen anyway—the destruction of capitalism and the creation of a workers' government. In his "Call for an American Writers' Congress" in the *New Masses* of January 22, 1935, Granville Hicks characterized the radical writer as one who did not "need to be convinced of the decay of capitalism, of the inevitability of revolution." Hicks's radical was a writer committed in every sense. Enter, into this scene of left-wing confidence, Kenneth Burke.

Burke remembers leaving the convention and overhearing one woman saying to another: "yet he looked so *honest*."[2] He remembers Joseph Freeman, one of the moving forces of the congress, standing up and saying, "We have a traitor among us!"[3] There is no record of Freeman's remark in the edited transcript of the discussion that was appended to the published proceedings of the congress; a remark does survive linking Burke's thought to Hitler's. However hysterical and inaccurate, however fictive or real these statements—those in print, those in Burke's memory— these reactions to Burke form one of the incontrovertible signs of the social effect of his critical writing and a hint that when Burke speaks the issues of the text involve a great deal more than pleasure.

The discourse that produced these startling effects on the official left of the 1930s was cunningly entitled "Revolutionary Symbolism in America." In those years of Marxist history (Gramsci was Mussolini's dying prisoner in 1935), Burke's speech had the discomforting feel of ideological deviance. Revolutionary *symbolism?* That is to confuse mere superstructural effect with the directive forces at the base, the economic motor principle of revolution. In *America*? That is to put on the blinders of nationalism which will prevent us from seeing the real world-historical dimension of revolution. Was Burke forgetting one of the key Hegelian points of Marx's theory of history: that the process moves inexorably from the local to the global? To stand with the intellectual left in the United States in the early 1930s was to stand in a place where Burke's kind of Marxism could be received only as heresy—as the very discourse of excrement.

Burke opens his essay by reminding his radical audience that principles of collectivity, whatever their genetic relation to a society's mode of production, do not themselves possess "primary reality" from a "strictly materialist point of view."[4] In effect what he does in the essay as a whole is to rewrite and elaborate Marx's immensely suggestive first thesis on Feuerbach, which was itself a dialectical rewriting of materialism as it had been hitherto understood: the thing, reality, sensuousness, must not be conceived, Marx argued, as an object exterior (and opposed) to practice, to intellection, to subjectivity, but as *"sensuous human activity, practice,"* with "practice" now understood as an integrated and indivisible whole of physical, intellectual, and emotional coordinates.[5] Marx's first thesis on Feuerbach may stand as a proleptic warning to all economist and mechanistic reductions of historical materialism to the mere materialism that would be performed in his name. The central paralyzing conflict in the history of Marxism may be located in its repetitious, even compulsive staging of that agon. With hindsight, we can see Burke's participation at the first American Writers' Congress in such an intellectual theater, with Burke enacting the father's role of historical materialist and his hostile respondents playing the parts of purists, sons anxious to purge all idealistic and therefore, of course, all fascist misappropriations of the master's word. By "strictly materialist point of view" Burke refers not, I believe, to the doctrine of historical materialism but to the historically conventional materialism of determinist character that Marx regarded as less intelligent than all-out idealism.

Although I think Burke one of the really superior readers of Marx and would place him among the group Perry Anderson called the "Western Marxists" (Anderson himself did not), it is not my purpose to suggest that Burke, not his respondents, best understood Marx. That sort of reading of the American Writers' Congress would only repeat and enforce another of the hopelessly infertile and claustrophobic dialogues within Marxism: "What did Marx really say, and who among us is the most faithful to his sacred books?" It appears to me that Burke's trouble with thirties Marxists in the United States stems from his deviant understanding of Marx—and by "deviant" I mean that Burke was doing something like New Left analysis within the anti-intellectualist, Second International intellectual context of the old left. One of his most significant contributions to Marxist theory (beyond his lonely American performance of "Western Marxism") is his pressing of the difficult, sliding notion of ideology, bequeathed to us by *The German Ideology*, out of the areas of intellectual trickery and false consciousness and into the politically productive textual realms of practical consciousness—rhetoric, the literary, and the media of what he tellingly called "adult education in America." The political work of the hegemonic, as

well as that of a would-be counter-hegemonic culture, Burke saw
(as Marx did not) as most effectively carried through at the level
of a culture's various verbal and nonverbal languages. In 1935
Burke was saying to America's radical left not only that a potentially revolutionary culture should keep in mind that revolution
must be culturally as well as economically rooted, but, as well,
and this was perhaps the most difficult of Burke's implications for
his radical critics to swallow, that a revolutionary culture must
situate itself firmly on the terrain of its capitalist antagonist, must
not attempt a dramatic leap beyond capitalism in one explosive,
rupturing moment of release, must work its way through capitalism's language of domination by working cunningly within it,
using, appropriating, even speaking through its key mechanisms
of repression. What Burke's proposal in 1935 to America's intellectual left amounts to is this: the substance, the very ontology of
ideology—an issue that Marx and Engels engaged with little
clarity, to put it charitably—in a broad but fundamental sense is
revealed to us *textually* and therefore must be grasped (read) and
attacked (reread, rewritten) in that dimension.

Burke concentrates therefore on the linguistic instruments
which produce our sense of community, the "symbols" of "communal relationship by which a group is bound," the "myth" of
the collective that is the "social tool for welding the sense of
interrelationship." Collective coherence is no psychic reflex of
the economy but the effect of an active, fusing work of cultural
production that organizes social cooperation—it is a "tool" that
"welds"—by disseminating those myths and symbols, stories
and words, which constitute our sense of ourselves in America as
part of a social whole presumably ministering justly and equita-
bly to its cooperative, individual subjects.[6] The primary lure of all
myths of collectivity is that they ask people to yield to what Burke
thinks a wholesome human tendency: the desire to give
ourselves to something beyond our isolate individual existences.
But, he quickly qualifies, and we can provide our own examples
of the danger, "the mere fact that the tendency is wholesome is
no guaranty that the people will not suffer for their wholesome-
ness."[7] As a radical American intellectual, with a keen awareness
of the liberal American political discourse of justice, equality, and
liberty, Burke says in so many words to the literary left gathered
in convention that an alternative discourse of justice, a socialist

discourse of equality and liberty, if it is successfully to supplant (uproot, plow under) the reigning hegemonic discourse of traditional America—if the socialist cause in America is to triumph, it will have to move inside and infiltrate the duplicitous but powerfully entrenched language of liberty to which we in the "land of the free" have already given allegiance. Burke's wager in 1935— and it is too soon to say that time has proved him wrong—was that the adhesive force of bourgeois nationalist symbols of allegiance was entering a state of decay, that other symbolic agencies were competing to take their place: that, indeed, this very situation of fluidity signified an unstable or revolutionary period in which people were in the process of shifting their allegiances from one myth to another. It was a situation of maximum opportunity for the literary intellectual: a struggle for cultural position was fully underway, and the literary intellectual, with his mastery of the tools of discourse, might have found himself in strategic leadership as a director of rhetorical war.

1

How then shall the writer speak? And to whom shall he direct his speaking? Those are the questions that preoccupy Burke as an intellectual; they are questions which, typically, he framed with his abiding concerns for history, rhetoric, power, tradition, and canon-formation. The "literary" for Burke is always embedded in those concerns. As a form of action in the world the literary is fully enmeshed in the social—it is not an imaginative space apart. This latter, however difficult a point to accept for those working from formalist traditions, should presumably have found a receptive audience at the first American Writers' Congress. Writing, not as haven for an isolated aesthetic pleasure, but as instrument for social change; the writer as "propagandist" (a word Burke understands in its full etymological history and which— unlike most professors of literature—he is not afraid to use or to apply to high-brow "literature").[8] What literary vulgarian, what socialist realist would not consent to those proposals? How could a convention of thirties radicals have received such a plea with hostility? Here is Burke's definition of the writer's task:

> Insofar as a writer is really a propagandist, not merely writing work that will be applauded by his allies, convincing the already convinced, but actually moving forward like a pioneer into outlying areas of the public and bringing them the first favorable impressions of his doctrine, the nature of his trade may give rise to special symbolic requirements. Accordingly, it is the propaganda aspect of the symbol that I shall center upon—considering the symbol particularly as a device for spreading the areas of allegiance.[9]

Burke's challenge to the Marxist intellectual ("Insofar as a writer is really a propagandist") is to stop making things easy for himself by talking into the mirror of the committed and to enter into dialogue with the uncommitted, the skeptical, even the hostile. His implied, bruising point—it was not misunderstood in 1935—was that the proletarian novel was both a literary and a political indulgence: applauded by the already convinced, unread by the working class, quietly alienating to the unconvinced, the proletarian novel took no risk of real dialogue. As intellectuals, proletarian writers and other Marxists, insofar as they are going to have a chance of disseminating doctrine, will have to move inward into examination of the rhetorical grounds of the dissemination of faith and simultaneously outward into critical scrutiny of the rhetorical structure of the dominant hegemony that inhibits the creation of new allegiances.

We can understand the hostility of American literary radicals to Burke's speech if we contextualize their feelings within the dramatic opposition that literary Marxists and formalists historically have tended to enact: Burke was asking his radical auditors to resist thinking of social doctrine as separable from its medium of dissemination. He was telling them that right social action, for a literary intellectual, was preeminently a literary act, because it was grounded in, its effectivity proceeded from, the rhetorical textures, strategies, and structures of discourse. The left intellectual represented, say, by Edmund Wilson, had trouble making an integral, internal connection between radical social vision and literary discourse. Cleanth Brooks, Wilson's thirties contrary, knew that and criticized Wilson on that score. But Brooks could

never see anything specifically political, left or right, in his formalist conception of the literary. The distinction and—to the old
left—the anomaly of Burke's mind was that it refused both sides
of this controversy; Burke simply negated and at the same time
preserved the Marxist/formalist controversy in a dialectical ma-
neuver that insisted that the literary was always a form of social
action, however rarely it might be recognized as such.

Burke moves from this general point about literary action to
the central social commitment of Marxism, the working class
itself. Taking a huge chance with this most sensitive of all Marxist
sentiments, he asks the intellectual left to consider the worker at
the symbolic—not the existential—level, as the embodiment of
an ideal, and then to weigh the rhetorical value of that symbol in
its American setting, and to measure the extent to which that
symbol is persuasively forceful, whether it disseminates revolution or perhaps something else, perhaps reaction. In effect Burke
asks Marxists—and the real value of his question is that it is not
limited to that audience—whether or not it is their ambition to
become workers: "There are few people who really want to work,
let us say, as a human cog in an automobile factory, or as gather-
ers of vegetables on a big truck farm. Such rigorous ways of life
enlist our *sympathies*, but not our *ambitions*. Our ideal is as far as
possible to *eliminate* such kinds of work, or to reduce its stren-
uousness to a minimum." Burke's nice point needs a little filling
out: you can't expect, he says, in effect, to his progressive friends,
on the one hand, to keep painting these riveting portraits of
workers under capitalism, of degradation and alienation—you
can't expect people to accept these portraits as the truth, which is
your rhetorical desire, after all, and then, on the other hand, at
the same time, expect people to want to identify with workers, or
become workers, or even enlist their energies of intellect and
feeling on behalf of workers. Even though your intention may be
otherwise, the fact is that your representations of workers are
being received as representations of "the other." Such portraits,
when they do enlist our sympathies, often, at the same time, in
ways too subtle to trace, create an effect of repulsion—which is
always, after all, the effect of "the other" when perceived from
inside the self-rationalizing norm. You must therefore attend to
the machinery of representation; you must, as Marx would urge,
rethink your representations of workers. You must somehow

bring them within, make sure that their fate and ours are bound up with each other. In cultural struggle, we try to seize the means of representation—rhetorical strategies and the media of their dissemination—and though this act is not equivalent to the seizing of the means of production, if we are successful the quixotic action generally involved in the latter will be unnecessary.[10]

If Burke could have cited *The German Ideology* in 1935—possible, but not likely—and if in addition he had known Jacques Derrida's Nietzschean critique of representation—likely, but not possible—he would have quoted the following sentences which crystallize (besides a Marx-Derrida connection that would later come to light) the heart of Foucault's message. Burke might have said to his audience: consider, in what I am about to quote, the surprising meanings of the words *represent* and *representative*, *universal* and *rational*; notice how these words, so epistemologically safe in their traditional setting, so isolated from the world of struggle, in their rationalist purity, are here involved as ideological weapons in the work of historical process and class warfare.

> For each new class which puts itself in the place of one ruling before it, is compelled, merely in order to carry through its aim, to represent its interest as the common interest of all members of society, that is, expressed in ideal form: it has to give its ideas the form of universality, and represent them as the only rational, universally valid ones. The class making a revolution appears from the very start, if only because it is opposed to a *class*, not as a class but as the representative of the whole of society; it appears as the whole mass of society confronting the one ruling class.

The embarrassing irony that Burke implicitly extracts from his analysis of the rhetorical effort of Marxism on behalf of the working class is that Marxist rhetoric emerges as reinforcement rather than as subversion of the hegemonic work of advanced capitalist society. "Some people," he says, and I take him—given his audience—to be referring to a certain type of left intellectual, "living overly sedentary lives, may like to read of harsh physical activity (as they once enjoyed Wild West fiction)—but Hollywood knows only too well that the people engaged in such kinds of effort are vitalized mainly by some vague hope that they may some day escape it."[11] Marxist rhetoric, in its effort to set in motion a counter-hegemony, must among other things project an image of a dehumanized and impoverished working class; the image is not rejected but welcomed by the intellectual forgers of the dominant hegemony who turn it against revolutionary intention. "Adult education in capitalist America," Burke writes, "today is centered in the efforts of our economic mercenaries (our advertising men and sales organizations) to create a maximum desire for commodities consumed under expensive conditions—and Hollywood appeals to the workers mainly by picturing the qualities of life in which this commercially stimulated desire is gratified."[12] The intention of what he calls adult education in America is to train or, in Foucault's sense, to *discipline* desire in the working class, to move it within a normalizing and self-perpetuating structure of desire promoted by an economic system that knows how to protect itself and, in this way, to move desire away from realizing one of its disruptive implications: the structural transformation of society and its socialist redefinition. Instead of foregrounding and pressing one of the potentially fatal internal contradictions of consumer capitalism, which would move it dialectically against itself (consumer capitalism must, through its manipulation of discourse and the image, "commercially stimulate" a desire for the good life whose social and economic historical ground cannot be capitalist society), Marxist rhetoric instead falls unwittingly into the hands of the artists and intellectuals of Madison Avenue and Hollywood and thereby helps to extend the historical life of consumer capitalism.

The "desire" that I refer to is not the ontological sort, the historically unlocated "lack" that Sartre defined in *Being and Nothingness*: it is, rather, that utopian yearning generated on the ground of capitalist economy itself, a yearning triggered by the message to the "free" laborer that, unlike his ancestor in the medieval system, *he* has unlimited social and economic fluidity—the message, to stay with my metaphor a moment longer, of "fluidity" itself. Especially in its democratic forms, capitalism creates radical desire as the possibility of unrestricted movement and personal fulfillment, socially and economically—a movement that was not permitted in the hardened hierarchy of the feudalist "structure." At the level of its own hegemonic metaphor, capitalism is no "structure." But since the capitalist system must resist the historical fulfillment of such desire—must resist socialism—if it is to preserve its inequitable (highly "structured") distribution of the fruits of labor, the system must find a way to appropriate the monster of utopian yearning for itself and thereby block the historical shift that Marx had predicted would follow upon its dialectically necessary deterioration.

Capitalism does find a way; it does block the teleology of history according to Marx. The first step was Frederick Taylor's, who disciplined workers' bodies for the ends of maximum productive efficiency; the second step was taken by consumer capitalism's poet-intellectuals who, in the media, discipline workers' desire through the creation and strategic deployment of the image—the media now understood not as a reflection of a preexistent economic base, and as therefore conspiratorially directed to promote acceptance of ruling class ideas, but as cultural mechanisms which produce the possibility of endless economic expansion by constituting, motivating, guiding, and "educating" desire. In its earlier stages, capitalism produces alienation; in its later, consumer, stage, it appropriates that alienation, turns its internal contradiction to advantage by projecting a perverse utopia of commodity-gratification that functions as the instrument for structuring desire as intention directed not toward the commodity per se but toward the capacity of the commodity to confer romance and wonder. Our novelists (Dreiser and Fitzgerald are among the most acute) have grasped the poetry of capitalist economics, but so have the creators of television commercials who portray drinking beer on a yacht not as what it is but as the fulfillment of desire—"going for the gusto." The perpetual production of the "new" commodity ensures, of course, that commodity-utopia will not be achieved, that desire is unappeasable, which is what consumer capitalism is all about: turning the potentially revolutionary force of desire produced on capitalist terrain toward the work of conserving and perpetuating consumer capitalism.

Consumer capitalism, therefore, direly needs the Marxist image of working class degradation, minus, of course, the Marxist analysis of the causes of that degradation; where Marxism says "exploitation," capitalism says a "condition" that its economic system will alleviate for those who work hard. If the motor principle of consumer capitalism is the production of both desire for the commodity and the illusion of potential gratification, a quality of happiness transcending commodities, though mediated by them, then proletarian fiction may unfortunately be one of the conditions of such production. The deep message of adult education in America is that the economic desire of workers can be requited only within a capitalist economy, undergirded and forever reinforced by its production of commodity-desire which, as Burke's reference to Hollywood's dream factory would suggest, well in advance of Guy Debord and Christopher Lasch, is synonymous with the production of the image. As critical theorist of social change, speaking to the intellectual vanguard of social change, Burke poses this question: "Is the symbol of the worker accurately attuned to us, as so conditioned by the reactionary forces in control of our main educational channels?" [13]

His response is no. But by answering in the negative Burke was not taking sides against Marx's historical wager on proletarian revolution; what he was denying, rather, was the rhetorico-symbolic value of the "worker," in discourses putatively aimed at changing minds for revolutionary ends, within an American social and political context in which class consciousness has been more or less successfully repressed. From the American point of view, the rhetorico-symbolic weight of the "worker" is burdened with an irrelevant historicity that is put into play every time the word is uttered, for it tends to carry with it an attendant rhetoric, decidedly foreign to our ways—*proletariat, bourgeoisie, ruling class*: the stuff of the European experience, but surely not of ours. Thus, along with the other disadvantages that Burke has noted, we have to add that all *talk* of a working *class* in America, or even just of *class*, and certainly of the complex awareness of hierarchical economic relations called class-*consciousness*, tends to sound forced, which is not to say that the experience of workers is a fantasy of Marxist intellectuals, or that the economic interests of a few do not require the exploitation of many. To say all of this against a Marxist rhetoric in the United States is not to speak against Marxism per se but only to acknowledge the awesomeness of the hegemonic discourse of our capitalist democracy. Lacking the bitter but useful historical consciousness of a precapitalist phase of American history, and saturated as we are by a mythology of equality ("one people," "indivisible," "with liberty and justice for all"), the symbol of the worker in America, with its Old World context of social hierarchy, not only does not embody our ideals (it cannot enlist our ambitions, as Burke put it), but, from a rhetorical point of view, when such a symbol is inserted into an American discourse on social change, it tends to have a fragmenting, not a unifying effect. The tragic effect of a traditional Marxist rhetoric in the American scene might be this: instead of extending (spreading, disseminating, propagating) a doctrine of revolutionary thought, a discourse weighted with symbols of proletarian life and exploitation might succeed only in isolating—I mean "quarantining"—workers' agony. Having thus inadvertently segregated workers from the social whole— irony of ironies for a totalizing philosophy—Marxist rhetoric then inadvertently plays into the purposes of the reactionary rhetoric poured out through our main educational channels where the worker is bombarded by images of the "good life," translated as maximum commodities consumed under expensive conditions. Maybe the bitterest of ironies to emerge from this conflict of rhetorics is not the quarantining effect of Marxist doctrine but the internal self-revulsion of workers as individuals and as members of an exploited group.

In suggesting that the American Marxist intellectual discard the symbol of the worker as rhetorical sine qua non of a vanguard movement, Burke by no means suggests that the real human costs extracted from workers be ignored or even down-played: "The rigors of the worker must certainly continue to form a major part of revolutionary symbolism, if only for the reason that here the worst features of capitalist exploitation are concentrated."[14] Burke is here urging that the rigors of the worker be inserted within a rhetorically more encompassing ("representative") symbol, so that the fate of the working class will be organically integrated with the fate of society as a whole: a vision of totality, undergirded by the working class, must be produced by a rhetoric of totality. The role of such rhetoric is not the persuasion of doubters that "there is" totality but the creation and insemination of a vision—we may say a heuristic fiction—whose promised child is consenting consciousness for radical social change. More specifically, what this counter-hegemonic effort entails is the choice of a central symbolism that would permit the vanguard intellectual to move with some hope for success into those very areas of society not disposed to think that the first order of American social business is structural change. Burke's suggestion, what created all the outrage and brought down on his head charges that he was a dupe of fascism who naively employed the rhetorical methods of Hitler, is that American Marxists choose in place of "the worker" the symbol of "the people."[15]

If it hopes to get its political work done in the United States, a Marxist rhetoric must take pains not to rupture itself from the historico-rhetorical mainstream of American social and political values. A truly ruptured rhetoric on behalf of the working class, standing in moral purity and isolation from the evils of all other political discourses, would not succeed in bringing the new society to birth ex nihilo but would only cut itself off from potentially sympathetic reception as it created not dialogue but narcissistic reflection. A radical rhetoric of revolution, instead of attempting to transcend the historical terrain of repression, should—I appeal to etymology here—work *at* the radical, within the history it would remake "at the root." The way out, if there is a way out, can only be the way through. Hence Burke's plea that "one cannot extend the doctrine of revolutionary thought among the lower middle class without using middle-class values—just as the Church invariably converted pagans by making the local deities into saints."[16] Burke's appeal to Marxists to immerse their rhetoric of revolution in the historical and cultural specificity of American folkways, to sink deeper into history, not to try to leap beyond it, though angrily rejected by his auditors at the American Writers' Congress, is primarily, I believe, a profound appeal to dialectics. Not dialectics as the theory of the gross institutional movement of social and economic history that Marx and Engels had outlined in *The German Ideology* but dialectics as a theory of the discursive movement of social and political history, dialectics as the theory of the emergent process of a liberating discourse—a dialectical rhetoric, not a simple negating language of rupture but a shrewd, self-conscious rhetoric that conserves as it negates. To a group presumably committed to the idea that revolution is made at the level of mind, and only executed, if at all, at the level of armed bodies, Burke is saying: get yourself a dialectical rhetoric and fashion it out of the stuff of the history and culture in which you find yourselves; in this way you will have the chance to be understood, clearly understood. That, to speak anachronistically, is the heart of Burke's Gramscian message—his appropriation of those decidedly non-teleological moments in the theory of history embedded in *The German Ideology*.

As dialectical rhetorician, the revolutionary writer must seize the historically persistent bourgeois rhetoric, somehow unmask its structure of oppression while preserving its emergent utopian intention. In America this means the appropriation, in the symbol of "the people," of a unifying direction, a latent ideal of society, "the ultimate *classless* feature which the revolution would bring about."[17] At the same moment, such appropriation must be a revelation of the frightening nationalistic and class prerogatives which hide their abusive force "behind a communal ideology." The ultimate point of such rhetoric is to create a new social center, aligned with the working class by its intellectuals— a critical mass galvanized into active "sympathy for the oppressed and antipathy towards our oppressive institutions."[18]

"The people" must be understood as an ideological element within an ideological system whose palpable, hegemonic form is linguistic. Burke is saying in effect that the discourse this element inhabits is not reducible to the interests of a specific class; nor, I would add, is it an epiphenomenon of the economic infrastructure of society. As an isolable element in the discourse, "the people," as a later critical theory would have it, is fundamentally "undecidable"; at the same time, from the systemic or ideological point of view, any ideological element necessarily plays a functionally determinate role. Burke in his address was saying that the literary seizing of the time involved, among other things, taking advantage of such latent undecidability by first extracting "the people" from its bourgeois nationalist system and then placing it onto a very different ideological terrain, one that it was not accustomed to occupying, where it could do the sort of very decidable work that the orthodox left then thought unimaginable. The function of the critical literary intellectual, Burke is arguing, is to engage in ideological struggle at the discursive level; to absorb and then rearticulate "the people" with a new organic ideology, where it might serve a different collective will. The fluidity, or undecidability, of the symbol is not, therefore, the sign of its social and political elusiveness but the ground of its historicity and of its flexible but also specific political significance and force.

Enabling this dialectical or historical work of rhetoric (the work of "argument") is one of the traditional resources of the rhetorician: the tropes, now manipulated not for ornamental purposes but for the ends of social change. The tropes must carry the argument of Marxism, which cannot be made "literally and directly" but only by the "intellectual company" it keeps. Literally and directly, the deployment of the general Marxist argument in the United States is subject to the same limitations that enervated the proletarian symbol—it appears foreign, disruptive to our culture's "unity" and "stability," an intruder into the "organic" social body. The revolutionary argument must be made implicitly, must be made to emerge as a necessary expression of our historical drift as a nation. Burke is urging a distinction between the work of the intellectual in his pamphleteering role, or in his role as political organizer—such work, in other words, that is explicit in its commitments—and the work of the intellectual as "imaginative" writer whose political contribution must be implicit. This distinction entails an unspoken judgment: Burke is betting that the writer's implied political alignment will ultimately do more effective political work because its literary-rhetorical matrix will make the force of radical vision difficult to resist.[19]

I think Burke is anticipating his later work on the connection between political authority and the tropes, the matter of "representation" in both its political and aesthetic meanings. The political, he is saying in so many words, must be embedded as a kind of synecdoche—as part of a larger cultural whole from which it cannot be extricated without violating the character of the whole, without also carrying out all the desirable features of the whole associated with it by necessity. That is the textual magic of synecdoche, and that is what Burke is getting at when he says that one's political alignment must be "fused" with "broader" cultural elements.[20] To "represent" the larger cultural whole as fused with a radical political alignment that functions as a synecdoche, a "representation" of the whole itself, is to naturalize the political, make it seem irresistible. This is the work of rhetoric, and rhetoric, like theory, as Burke knows, is not necessarily in the service of radical change.

Let me draw out the implication: the radical mind has no privileged mode of persuasion available to it; there is no morally pure, no epistemologically secure, no linguistically uncontaminated route to radical change. Thus Burke's chief example of implicit poetic strategy: "this is what our advertisers do when they recommend a particular brand of cigarette by picturing it as being smoked under desirable conditions; it is the way in which the best artists of the religious era recommended or glorified their faith; and I imagine it would be the best way of proceeding today."[21] To attempt to proceed in purity—to reject the rhetorical strategies of capitalism and Christianity, *as if such strategies were in themselves responsible for human oppression*—to proceed with the illusion of purity is to situate oneself on the margin of history, as the possessor of a unique truth disengaged from history's flow. It is to exclude oneself from having any chance of making a difference for better or for worse.

The traditional humanist response to all of this is not difficult to imagine: Isn't what you and Burke call Marxism at bottom, then, sheer and brutal Nietzschean will to power? Are you not saying that the end justifies the means? What, therefore, makes you think that your theory will not do to others what you say other theories have done? I used to think those questions powerfully sobering; I now think they are merely frightened, for they imply individually and collectively a desire for a transcendental guarantee that action in this world can proceed in innocence, with no harm done on any side—a desire, in other words, to know in advance that what we do can produce only good. Of course those who pose such questions know better—that is why they do nothing, and in such quietude assume that they do no harm. The means of rhetoric, in fact, are neither good nor bad: they simply are.

The intellectual who would be self-consciously socially effective can but proceed, then, in the hegemonic mode, creating consensus. Consensus cannot be created by the purist stance of "antithetical morality," and that is what is at stake in Burke's suggestion that the symbol of the worker be replaced by an encompassing symbolism whose rhetorical force will be located on the common ground, the kindred values it "finds," by sleight of hand, for writer and audience, for only within such a rhetorical relation, so structured by commonality of value and purpose, is the reception of radical values possible. Here is Burke on the rhetorical conditions of propagation:

> Particularly as regards the specific problems of propaganda, the emphasis upon the *antithetical* tends to incapacitate a writer for his task as a *spreader* of doctrine by leading him too soon

into antagonistic modes of thought and expression. It gives him too much authority to condemn—and however human this desire to grow wrathful may be, and however justified it is by the conditions all about us, the fact remains that his specific job as a propagandist requires him primarily to wheedle or cajole, to practice the arts of ingratiation. As a propagandizer, it is not his work to convince the convinced, but to plead with the unconvinced, which requires him to use *their* vocabulary, *their* values, *their* symbols, insofar as this is possible.[22]

Dialectics as rhetoric, as art of ingratiation—as *"propaganda by inclusion"*: the creation, in a revolutionary era, when symbols of allegiance are being exchanged, of a revolutionary symbolism.[23] "Revolutionary" means fundamentally for Burke "transitional"—the state, both historically and psychologically, of being "between" and, fiction of all radical fictions, the state of "tendency," of being "on the way." It is not a question of whether there is a teleology in history—a question for metaphysicians and some Marxists—but a question of forging the rhetorical conditions for change, a question of forging (and I'll insist on the Joycean resonance of that term) a teleological rhetoric, of creating, through the mediations of such discourse, a collective will for change, for moving history in the direction for our desire. We need a rhetoric, Burke concludes, that creates a psychological bridge, a Janus-faced language; "looking both forwards and back" it establishes—forges—its historicity, its continuity as the inevitable, emergent language—fiction of tendency— -and by so doing becomes as well the Janus-faced psychological bridge that carries "the people" smoothly, without break, from bourgeois democratic location to the state of socialism.[24] This political symbolism becomes effective when it is surrounded by the fullest of cultural textures—when one's political alignment is associated with "cultural awareness in the large."[25] At such a moment, the war for cultural position will have been won and the hegemony in place, replaced.

One of the chapters of a full-scale history of Marxist thought will have to be on Kenneth Burke who, among other things, was doing Gramsci's work before anyone but Gramsci (and his censors) could read what would be called the *Prison Notebooks*. The real force of Burke is not limited, however, to his historically independent Gramscian practice or to his American discovery of the popular front. The real force of his thinking is to lay bare, more candidly than any writer I know who works in theory, the socially and politically enmeshed character of the intellectual. To put it that way is to say that Burke more even than Gramsci carries through the project on intellectuals implied by parts of *The German Ideology*. And Burke did this not just occasionally but repeatedly over a career that has spanned more than sixty years.

2

The great theoretical antagonist of the themes Burke launched in his address to the American Writers' Congress was no one in attendance, but a writer whose work began making its considerable impact much later, in the late 1960s and early 1970s—a writer who, by the end of the 1970s, might have laid just claim, had he so desired, to being the undisputed master in the United States of what is called deconstruction. I refer to Paul de Man, of course, whose two collections, *Blindness and Insight* (1971) and *Allegories of Reading* (1979), represent the most subtle and influential efforts in the deconstructive mode in English and perhaps in any language—and I do not except the work of Jacques Derrida. We speak easily these days of "Derrideans" and "deconstructors" (interchangeable terms) but when the dust kicked up by recent critical skirmishes finally settles, we may well see that the dominant literary-critical movement of the American 1970s was "de Manian," that the two collections of essays I've just cited provided a reading machine for his disciples: the models of deconstructive strategy, the terminology, the idea of literature and literary history, and (perhaps the most telling sign of all of de Man's dominance) even a certain turn of critical phrasing, a prose style for more than one generation of those graduate students, often the very brightest, with committed interests in criticism.

In an essay of 1973 called "Semiology and Rhetoric," in which he explicitly showcased the deconstructive strategy for the American scene with readings of Proust, Yeats, and the discourse of

Archie Bunker, de Man predicted that all of literature would respond in similar fashion to his techniques of reading and that "in fact" it would be the future task of literary critics to take on this very job of deconstructive application—in effect, the miming of himself as critical father, with the canon pretty much left intact but reread and therefore reconstituted in the light of deconstruction.[26] De Man's prediction has come true. The most valuable product of deconstruction's current critical hegemony may not, however, be the reprocessing (allegorizing) of the literary canon by the sons and daughters of de Man, who to this point show not a trace of the anxiety of influence, but the critical war between "traditional" and "new" critics which this redoing has touched off. I have argued elsewhere that the differences between traditionalists and the newest generation of New Critics, though real, have been exaggerated by the contending parties. This exaggeration of difference, on the other hand, has been extremely useful to the warriors involved because it has drawn much attention to themselves and their putative opposition. But the differences may be no greater than those separating Republicans and Democrats. Unlike Kenneth Burke and the commitment he represents, traditionalists and New Critics are alike committed to the security of literature, and they share a common foreign policy: both parties stand up for the literary canon as we have known it (New Critics would add a few philosophers to the list); both parties stand up for the notion of literary autonomy, however differently that autonomy may be defended, defined, and located; both stand up for the segregation of the literary and political functions of the intellectual. The war between traditionalists and deconstructors will, I'll predict, draw to a close by the end of this decade, and the making of peace will be founded upon a discovered consensus of values. The differences then between traditionalists and deconstructors will be about the same as those which obtain between the old Yale New Critics and traditionalism.

If de Man now represents a rupturing figure for traditionalist critics and scholars, a dangerous radical, later, after the accord, I would wager that he will be rediscovered as the most brilliant hero of traditionalism, the theorist who elaborated the cagiest argument for the political defusion of writing and the intellectual life. I have tried to make the case for Burke's address to the

American Writers' Congress as an exemplary effort by the humanist intellectual to insert the theoretical, the philosophical, and, in the broadest sense, the literary, into the political process. Burke's intervention is the theorizing of the act of intervention itself; I'm not sure that his specific example will in the end be especially central; I'm convinced that his model for strategic linkage is indispensable. In de Man I think we see something like an attempt at the ultimate subversion of what Burke stands for—not the breaking of the link (the link can never be broken) but a demonstration that the fact of linkage is insignificant because what linkage makes possible, intervention itself, can make no difference: for de Man, to intervene or not to intervene is no question at all. The insidious effect of his work is not the proliferating replication of his way of reading—a point often lamented by traditionalist critics—but the paralysis of praxis itself: an effect that traditionalism, with its liberal view of the division of culture and political power, should only applaud. I am saying that the deconstruction of deconstruction will reveal, against apparent intention, a tacit political agenda after all, one that can only embarrass deconstruction, particularly its younger proponents whose activist experiences within the socially wrenching upheavals of the 1960s and early 1970s will surely not permit them easily to relax, without guilt and self-hatred, into resignation and ivory tower despair.

From the existentialism and phenomenology of his early career to the Derrideanism of his most recent essays, reports of changes in de Man's thinking (including my own) may be exaggerated. It may be that all attempts to see him as an exponent of contemporary philosophy and theory are fundamentally mistaken because it may be that de Man is more an exemplary instance than an exponent, and a singularly distinct instance at that. There is a radical continuity in his thought that revises as it illuminates a radical continuity in the philosophical tradition of Hegel, Nietzsche, Heidegger, the Sartre of *Being and Nothingness*, and Derrida—these figures in the modern Continental tradition are not called upon by de Man as sources and models of right thinking; they are distilled for an essence that his alchemy alone thus far seems capable of feigning. De Man makes the modern Continental tradition in philosophy deliver an astonishing political lesson, generally not associated with it but probably appropriate nevertheless. The essence of the lesson is signified by the most privileged epistemic term in his vocabulary: the term is "lucidity," and the consequences of his meditation on this term for the life of praxis are corrosive.

In his Harvard dissertation of 1960, de Man clarifies the figure in his critical carpet. Through a series of unparalleled analyses of Mallarmé, the Mallarmé of the recent critical scene shows us that "lucidity" depends upon self-knowledge; that the self known in self-knowledge is grasped in an act of pure inwardness whose intentional object is withdrawn from all public gaze and all the demands and determinacies of collectivity. In an aside against Marxists, de Man asserts that collectivity is a "dodge" from the problems of "individual" consciousness. Simultaneously, and subversively, what is grasped in inward-directed meditation— and here is de Man's critical appropriation, before Derrida, of the Cartesian moment—is the ironic structure of all epistemic desire for lucidity. De Man argues that the quest for lucidity will reveal this metatruth about truth—that it "can only exist as an intent that fails." So much for self-knowledge and the problems of "individual" consciousness. The implication of this failure for de Man's literary theory is that the "ultimate form"—he means literary form—will describe a mode that he will later call self-deconstruction, for it is a form which "must contain its negation, concretely inscribed into the form itself."[27] Such a form will function as a kind of linguistic simulacrum, a representation in language of that failed, nonlinguistic interior quest for light. In de Man's dissertation, "literature" earns its value by imaging forth the negative truth of human failure, a truth apparently structured into its very being: human being as failure. Negative epistemology mimes negative ontology. This early version of a deconstructed, fissured subject that can never know itself will set up de Man's early attack on Marxism, in which the Marxist call for engagement is held to a standard that de Man's own remarks on lucidity and self-knowledge make impossible to live up to. In a critical allusion to Sartre's Marxism of *littérature engagée*, he says that the way "to be present to one's time begins in total inwardness, certainly not out of indifference towards history, but because the urgency of one's concern demands a lucid self-insight; action will follow from itself, when this insight has been gained."[28]

The wholly interiorized self of de Man's analysis needs, as he would say, "to be put into question." So questioned, we quickly see revealed the triumphant production of idealist philosophy in the early bourgeois era—the private, enclosed self (*res cogitans*) whose location in subjective substance outside the social ensures what de Man's language will not in 1960, or now, confront: that no action can follow from a "lucid self-insight" because the product of such insight (a leit-motif in the dissertation) is the repetitious awareness of the socially uncontaminated poetic mind that it is powerless to achieve its intention to know itself and to ground action on such knowledge, its awareness that poetic force will always be frustrated and that one will keep on pursuing epistemological impossibility and thereby ensure a career of failure. In the "light" of self-insight we learn that no lucidity is possible—here is the basis of de Man's epistemology of failure. Once such epistemic certainty is established, he suggests, action is supposed to follow "from itself" almost naturally. But epistemic certainty, whether negative or positive, is not a logical condition for action, for one thing. For another, after such knowledge as de Man's—of the mind eternally frustrated in its intention to know itself—a key affective condition for action has been destroyed: the modest feeling of confidence that the effects of one's "doing" will not be defeated in advance. But how, really, can "doing" in the historical world be defeated in advance, since effects are always phenomena of the future, the history that is to be? De Man can know what he knows because in his theory of history there is no future, no temporal vista really open, no possibility not always already snuffed by epistemic failure. The idealist dream of a self-substance within, a substance that prevails, turns into the nightmare of nihilism when the longed-for substance lapses unsubstantial in the cruel light of criticism; that is the philosophical narrative implied by de Man's brilliant analyses of irony and rhetoric. But the end of idealism is also the point of departure for quite another kind of critical theory—one that is never tempted to find a rock of authority "inside," that does not play nostalgia in the mask of irony, that does not find in nihilism the alternative to failed idealism.

De Man's requirement of lucidity is rooted in the contemplative tradition of classical philosophy; pressed too hard, as he presses, the need for lucidity re-establishes a classic problem of classical philosophy: the unbridgeable gap between knowledge and action, the world of being and the world of becoming. In de Man's practice the contemplative tradition in philosophy falls prey to the illness of the spirit to which it is traditionally prone, *acedia*, the overly scrupulous concern over what one ought to do, which prevents one from doing anything at all. The dominant metaphor for *acedia* in his most recent work on rhetoric is "paralysis." He means the paralysis of action, underwritten by an aporia "between trope and persuasion" which will deny lucidity to the intellect and guarantee in the end that no mind knows what it is doing—no mind, apparently, except de Man's, which lucidly knows that no lucidity is possible.[29]

The most significant essay in *Blindness and Insight* on this political issue of action, "Literary History and Literary Modernity" (1969), works through an argument that structures the theorizing of de Man's later essays collected in *Allegories of Reading*, even though there the key terms, "literary" and "modernity," tend to be replaced and subsumed by the term "rhetoric." The very title of "Literary History and Literary Modernity" indicates a formalist intention—this is a work, apparently, about the principles of the self-contained realm of literature; no theory of history at large or of society is implied. On the other hand, there is that last clever paragraph of the essay, which in the most tentative phrasing puts forth the most teasing and most instigating of propositions—not lost on his disciples—that the paradigm for literature he has constructed is not only the paradigm for literary history but also the paradigm for "history in general," and particularly for those "texts" that "masquerade in the guise of wars or revolutions."[30] The examples cited—incited—wars or revolutions, are, like all of de Man's examples, not innocent. Not only are books "texts" but everything is a text, there is nothing outside the text, as Derrida put it, and all texts are "problematic." This absolutization of language by structuralism and poststructuralism has been challenged and shown to be wanting in a recent series of lectures given by Perry Anderson at Irvine. I want to explore, however, not the logical weaknesses of that position—Anderson has done that—but the political effect of assuming it.

De Man begins by offering a series of tentative definitions: "modernity" is neither primarily fashion nor literary style but

"spontaneity," a "way of acting or behaving"; concepts of "literature" and "history" must therefore stand in necessary conflict
with modernity, since they denote reflection, ideas, memory, the
past.[31] "History," then, along with terms like "classical" and
"traditional," is the antonym of modernity, even if—and this
qualification will quickly become a leading theme—even if the
term "modernity" is itself antique, with a history dating back at
least to the fifth century.[32] With that philological aside and the
soon-to-be-falsified opposition of history and modernity in place,
the stage is set for the entrance of Nietzsche, mentor of poststructuralists, whose meditation "On the Use and Abuse of History"
functions as one of the sacred books of recent theory. De Man
begins his reading of Nietzsche by noting an initial opposition
and a desperately posited sense for the term "modernity." Nietzsche opposes history to modernity, but his most far-reaching
meaning for "modernity" is "life," by which he understands
health, vitality, energy, action, and the capacity to act: "life,"
then, as creativity, origin, presence and the present, as opposed
to the past and the future.[33]

Whether he intended it or not, de Man's analysis of the relation of the terms life and history in Nietzsche quickly shades into
political allegory. Genuine humanity exists in, de Man argues,
depends upon, an "absolute forgetting" that is "the condition for
action"; absolute forgetting is the "radical impulse" standing
behind all modernity.[34] The "condition for action" is not just
forgetting—which is Nietzsche's modest point, but (de Man's
inflation of the Nietzschean point) an "absolute" forgetting, a
pleonastic underscoring that hints at de Man's fundamental hostility toward the political, a stacking of the cards against action's
political efficacy. What can "absolute forgetting" really mean?
Forgetting is nothing if not a dialectical term: its force depends
upon a *remembering* that must be repressed, and repression is not
the same as "absolute forgetting"; remembering demands a
forgetting, a dialectical process foreign to animals, so Nietzsche
and de Man assume, and that is why animals are stupidly content. De Man and Nietzsche both know well the dialectics of
forgetting; de Man in fact argues that Nietzsche's most interesting moments move against—that is, "deconstruct"—the opposition of history and life by showing them to be involved with each
other in an interdependent relationship of nonopposition. This

relationship can and will be called ironic, paradoxical, puzzling, curious, undecidable—in short, an "aporia."[35] For there is no "absolute forgetting": it is an illusion, and a moment's worth of reflection will be enough to convince us that this is so.

But since de Man has forced this naive illusion to be "the condition for action," what then of action? In his summation of this part of his analysis of Nietzsche, the specific content of his latent political allegory has to do with the phenomenon of revolution. If only an "absolute forgetting" can be the basis of the "radical impulse" (what de Man calls "modernity" and Nietzsche "life"), if only "absolute forgetting" can be the basis, the very "condition" of action, and "absolute forgetting" is an illusion, then de Man, through an unprecedented reading of Nietzsche, is implicitly developing a discourse against radical action and revolution and, more extremely, a discourse against action and change in general. From the displaced point of view of traditional psychoanalysis, an "absolute forgetting" would constitute a symbolic parricide, a desire to destroy personal genealogy and to be reborn with an original identity. From the sociohistorical point of view, an "absolute forgetting" would constitute a collective social desire to destroy the genealogical process of history and to be reborn, in the revolutionary moment, in a society ruptured from the past, with an identity that owes nothing to the past. If we accept de Man's premise that "absolute forgetting" is the "condition for action," however, we are not only forced into his implied conclusions about radicalism and revolution—his argument also moves logically against action and change of any sort, because their condition, too, he has stipulated, is "absolute forgetting." De Man's unprecedented reading of Nietzsche puts Nietzsche on the side of the moribund herd mentality.

Nietzsche's hatred of history is anyway only a front, de Man believes, for his deep-rooted "pessimism," his "sense of historical causality," his genealogical theory of history as a generative "chain" that fatally links present, past, and future in an indissoluble process.[36] A truly achieved modernity, in the undialectical sense of the word, would be severed not only from the past but also from the present and the future; such modernity would be the achievement of transcendent irrelevance. Moving thus forcefully against modernity in that sense, against the simplest versions of aestheticism and formalism, both de Man and de Man's Nietzsche, at the same time, in the same gesture, burden their thought with a peculiar historical weight that, in the end, may be the basis of an ultimate savage torpor. As de Man writes: "Nietzsche sees no assurance that his own reflective and historical attempt achieves any genuine change, he realizes that his text itself can be nothing but another historical document."[37] Modernity and history relate to each other in a "curiously contradictory way that goes beyond antithesis or opposition"—and this "curious contradiction," which de Man calls an "aporia," is what precludes "genuine change," a phrase that must be translated in de Man's discourse with phrases from other places in the essay ("radical renewal," "new departure," "true present," and "new origin"), phrases which the drift of his logic would force us to conclude are synonymous with "genuine change."[38] Again de Man's pleonasm is politically resonant: what would be an "old origin"?

Let me repeat and extend the logical structure of de Man's implied political discourse. If "absolute forgetting" is the "condition for action," then, with the discovery that "absolute forgetting" is impossible, any "action" (de Man defines it as the "unmediated free act that knows no past") becomes an illusion; not only do the radical products of action become impossible, but so do changes understood as *differences*.[39] Only revolutionary changes would qualify as "genuine," in de Man's definition of that word, but they cannot occur on the terrain of history—and the terrain of history is inescapable. So any historically situated change less dramatic than rupture with the past is not genuine— is no change at all. Though it will take me the remainder of this book to argue it with any fullness, I'll say here in passing that the problem is with the theory of history that frames de Man's writing. This theory deliberately presses upon political practice a naive meaning that de Man has cleverly insinuated into his general concepts of action and change. But no mature political thinker I know, certainly not Marx or any of his significant inheritors, would accept such theories of history, action, and change. "Simple rupture" is a rhetorical notion de Man needs in order to construct his own notions of literature and history and to debunk Marxism in the same act.

With Nietzsche's help, de Man is now ready to put forth his idea of literature and literary history. In the paradoxical as distinguished from the naive sense of modernity, literature, he declares, "has always been essentially modern."[40] In one stroke "literature" and "literary history" are identified in an essentialist and synchronic concept ("essentially," "always"). Literature/ literary history not only contains specific aporias; its very being constitutes the sign of the aporia: literature /literary history is the exemplary structure of the aporia. For what de Man calls "literature" (others might say more modestly "romantic literature") has an affinity with action as the creation of an origin ("the unmediated free act that knows no past"), but—problematically—"literature" is simultaneously and "always" a reflection upon the act. In this way literature "both affirms and denies its own nature or specificity" as creativity, originality, modernity.[41] "Literature, which is inconceivable without a passion for modernity," also appears *internally* opposed, fissured by a "subtle resistance to this passion."[42] De Man formulates his point by appealing to two phrases he culls from Baudelaire—"représentation du présent," "mémoire du présent"—which, as he says, express the aporia of the literary in that they combine a "repetitive with an instantaneous pattern"—the sense of openness and freedom of a present severed from all temporal dimensions but at the same time integrated within a large historical perspective, "a sense of totality and completeness."[43] The illusion of action in de Man's analysis now modulates into the illusion of the man of action ("a man of the moment, severed from past and future").[44]

If we should ask de Man what deconstructs "action" and the "man of action"—modernity, radical renewal, genuine change, revolution—he must answer "literature" or "literary history." With Baudelaire, he will conclude that "the attraction toward an action, a modernity, and an autonomous *meaning* that would exist outside the realm of language . . . is primarily an attraction to what is not art."[45] For de Man there is nothing, finally, that can't be processed in his literary categories. In his definition of literature, the old New Critics' idea of the autonomous poem, "the poem in itself," yields to the autonomous intertext, literary history, and the intertext of literary history is the production of a nexus of three moments: the desire for rupture, or flight—first moment; the falling back into the clutches of history, or the return—second moment; and de Man's prized moment, the third moment of the aporia—"the turning point at which flight changes into return or vice-versa."[46] This moment of the aporia, which is the object of all deconstructive criticism, requires the two previous moments of flight and return. Those two moments in turn require politically inhibiting concepts which suffocate the possibility of a social change that would not be either the mere illusion of change, mere repetition, or would not presume to be an origin separated from history. The two unacceptable concepts—fundamental presuppositions, really—are, first, the concept of history that de Man deploys synchronically with terms like "completeness" and "totality," a concept that would deny any real meaning to the idea of the "possible" as a force emerging from the fundamental historical process. If, as Gramsci says, possibility means "freedom," then de Man's implicit denial of the "possible" is an implicit affirmation of determinism.[47] This is the concept of history that undergirds the moment of return. I refer, second, to the concept of action—the moment of flight—which depends, for the meaning of "rupture" de Man has given it, and has shown to be naive, on the negation of the second, or historical-determinist moment. So by putting together two moments which in themselves are unacceptable to him, to Nietzsche, and to any mature thinker roughly in the Marxist tradition, de Man creates his promised land, the third moment of the aporia.

What now is the point of this definition of literature as literary history? As he moves toward his point, de Man's discourse again shades into political allegory. His aporia cannot escape his key antecedent, a fatalistic theory of history. I say that such a theory is the key antecedent because it is the necessary driving force of the desire for rupture. In decidedly elegiac tones, de Man asserts that the "literary mode of being" is a "form of language that knows itself to be mere repetition, mere fiction and allegory, forever unable to participate in the spontaneity of action and modernity."[48] How curious that action and modernity, which were shown to be naive illusions, now become objects of nostalgia, signs of a political desire for a "radical renewal" that was also shown to be naive: the claim for modernity, for a new beginning, "turns out to be the repetition of a claim that has always already been made."[49] The aporia of literary structure, moreover, is reflected in the writer's attitude—we can call it an aporia of feeling, for the "same fatal interplay governs the writer's attitude toward modernity."[50] The fatalistic moment of history, de Man's second moment, becomes generalized and lifted up into the third moment—"the fatal interplay"—and this moment of aporia now constitutes the most inclusive fatality of literary history: the "literary" moment must repeat itself through the synchronic history of "literature." Hence the "distinctive character of litera- ture . . . becomes manifest as an inability to escape from a condi- tion that is felt to be unbearable."[51] Which is to say, at a minimum, that the "distinctive character of literature," what it has "always" and "essentially" been, constitutes for the literary mind a matrix of despair, resignation, futility, frustration, fatalism, cynicism, and hopelessness—all good feelings for underwriting, whether or not by intention, the status quo of the literary world.

If this minimal claim were all that was at stake in de Man's argument, if his conception of the literary world truly segregated the literary from all involvement, there would be no need to confront his argument. De Man writes easily within the claus- trophobic space of the literary man, but that is a deception; his ambitions have never been those self-trivializing ones of the simple formalist. Let me quote his last sentence: "If we extend this notion beyond literature, it merely confirms that the bases for historical knowledge are not empirical facts but written texts, even if these texts masquerade in the guise of wars or revolutions."[52] Despite the caution of its phrasing this sentence does insert the literary into history at large—and such insertion has the effect of transforming history at large into the literary: de Man's own literary heritage, from Blake to Wilde, makes itself felt. What the sentence says, first, is that since we can only interpret history, so-called empirical facts (like a language) must be structured by the reader—we "read" them as texts. That is an unobjectionable point, a lasting truth of structuralism's legacy which is interesting and useful, however, only if we can make distinctions between verbal texts and other languages of social interaction. But de Man is claiming a good deal more than the structuralist truism. He is saying that history is not merely a text, that the text of history is not merely an imitation of literature. He is saying that history is an imitation of what he has defined as the literary. To say this is to make the maximal claim, and what is necessarily involved in such a claim is the transference, or projection, of all those paralytic feelings of the literary onto the terrain of society and history. There is nothing outside the text, said Derrida; de Man revises to say there is nothing outside the literary text. What de Man's claim carries, given his definition of the literary as massive ("fatal") persistence, is the postulation of the most genuine meaning of political conservatism. This, I think, is what de Man is teaching; this is the effect of his theory; this is his social work; this is the message of poststructuralism in the United States.

The "lucid" epistemological brooding of de Man is not the radical philosophic gesture it is often made out to be. Richard Rorty's *Philosophy and the Mirror of Nature* will help us to place it as a continuation, however ironic, of the ahistorical work of traditional philosophy that has now moved into its elegiac phase. Deconstruction brings the news that all hope for securing the "foundations" of knowledge is futile—that foundations must be replaced by "abysses," that "representations" must always be "put into question." But the rhetorical force of de Man's deconstructive work requires our misplaced faith in those very foundations and representations—which is to say that the work of deconstruction rests on the very vocabulary of knowledge-as-representation that it would subvert. Instead of "setting aside" the discourse of representation, in a Copernican move, by replacing it (as did Nietzsche and William James, for example) with a discourse of knowledge as action and power, as a tool always at work within specific historical situations, as always ideologically freighted, deconstruction chooses to stay within the traditional paradigm of transcendental representation, finding its distinctive project in the necessarily endless demonstration that representations fail to do what they say they do. Deconstruction's useful work is to undercut the epistemological claims of representation, but that work in no way touches the real work of representation—its work of power. To put it another way: deconstruction can show that representations are not and cannot be adequate to the task of representation, but it has nothing to say about the social work that representation can and does do. Deconstruction confuses the act of unmasking with the act of defusing, the act of exposing epistemological fraud with the neutralization of political force. Deconstruction, then, is a "critical" philosophy, but only in the slimmest sense of the word—it may tell us how we deceive ourselves, but it has no positive content, no alternative textual work to offer to intellectuals. It has nothing to say. Maybe that makes it the best sign of all of where the American humanist intellectual stands today: feeling vaguely out of it, desiring change, but crushed, stifled, and enervated by the fear that the robust, active will may not succeed.

Politically, deconstruction translates into that passive kind of conservatism called quietism; it thereby plays into the hands of established power. Deconstruction is conservatism by default—in Paul de Man it teaches the many ways to say that there is nothing to be done. The mood is all from early T. S. Eliot. We are Prufrocks all, all hollow men, who inhabit the wasteland that we know now is the humanities wing of the modern university: "Paralyzed force, gesture without motion." Dante would have cast us into the vestibule of hell as comrades of those outcasts who took no sides in the rebellion. Am I too harsh with de Man's work? In the course of this book it will be clear that what I am most critical of in de Man is not something freakish but, rather, something central to the way academic humanists tend to perceive themselves. There is a de Man in us all. For similar unsettling reasons, like Borges he is one of our representative men. One of the great things about Burke is that he knew the truths of de Man early, and he knew them without the disastrous political consequences that seem everywhere to track de Man and his students. The subject belongs to Henry James: there is a moment in "The Jolly Corner," a pivotal moment for that story, and for mine, in which one of James's characters broods over the question of his inaction. And the brooding turns quickly into agony over the awareness that the paralysis of inaction is doubled in the consciousness of such. "Oh to have this consciousness was to *think*—and to think . . . as he stood there, was, with the lapsing moments, not to have acted! Not to have acted—that was the misery and the pang—was even still not to act; was in fact *all* to feel the thing in another, in a new and terrible way." Yes, but "The Jolly Corner" has a happy ending.

I want to contest the Prufrockian mood of current critical sophistication, to say that we need not align ourselves with either

Dante's pathetic outcasts, who could not choose, or with those whom Martin Luther King called "moderates," who would not choose. The first question before us is not whether we are going to be Marxists, but whether or not, and on what ground, the examined life is worth living.

Part Two

Until recent years the canons of truth and sanity that govern the writing of critical theory in the United States have implicitly decreed that much of what Kenneth Burke does is a deviation from good sense. Which I translate: disturbing, different, perhaps dangerous. Burke is the great either/or of contemporary theory for he cannot be accepted in small, bearable doses. He must be taken all at once or not at all. But to take him all at once would require a radical reconception of the basis of what is usually called humanistic study. For about sixty years now Burke has been telling us that the conventional divisions of the humanities, with literature, philosophy, history, linguistics, and social theory each self-enclosed within the fortress-like walls of the disciplines, housing experts too often ignorant and contemptuous of everything outside their respective castles—this man without tenure, a Ph.D., or even a B.A., who writes books which cannot be touched by conventional academic definition, has been telling us that this is all, at best, a lie of administrative convenience and, at worst, a reinforcement in our institutions of higher education of the current hegemony of advanced capitalism. In order to approach Burke on something like his own terms, we (and I mean American academic intellectuals) need to cease reducing the richly integrated and socially urgent European conception of critical theory to the comfortably alienating ivory tower formalism of literary theory.

To enter such a domain of critical theory, we are first of all required to work through the critical philology of Raymond Williams, who reminds us that our narrow, sacralized term "literature" did not take its current meaning as "imaginative writing" until well into the eighteenth century; like Williams, Burke prefers a wider-ranging meaning and understands the sociopolitical import of the narrowed sense of the literary.[1] The tough road into Burke may be somewhat smoothed if, along with Williams's counsel, we bring some awareness of Foucault's late work, particularly in *Discipline and Punish*, which demonstrates, among many things about the emergence and character of modern society, that in the very moment in the later eighteenth century at which Williams pinpoints the crucial shift to the modernist sense of the literary, we can also discern the powerful entrenchment of a series of normalizing, disciplinary mechanisms in all the key institutions of our society (factories, schools, hospitals, the army). If we join the historical understanding of Williams with that of Foucault, we come out with something like the following: the refining by literary intellectuals in the late eighteenth century of the concept of the "literary" to mean "imaginative writing" becomes an inadvertent service on behalf of the coercive and even totalitarian tendencies of modern society—a way of supervising and containing the "literary" by keeping it enclosed in its own space, a mode of self-policing, as it were.

The segmentation of intellectual space along the lines of our currently recognized "disciplines," as they are established in our colleges and universities, is no picture of a natural compartmentalization of human capacities but of a will to control and dominate by dividing and partitioning—or so Foucault would argue. Burke's books respect no such academico-political arrangements. The man who said that his ideal of criticism was to "use all that there is to use" can give no comfort to disciplinary chauvinists.[2] Burke, or more plausibly the model of intellectuality that he represents, is the antidote, I would argue, within our various educational institutions for the cancer of the spirit portrayed by Foucault in *Discipline and Punish*. We may become intellectually comfortable with Burke's way if we keep in mind that he does not participate in the marked effort of literary theorists, again since the later eighteenth century, to denigrate rhetoric in order to elevate the imaginative; nor does he sympathize with the ancient (yet continuing) Platonic effort to exclude rhetoric from the realm of philosophy. For Burke, writing, including what we call the literary, is a discourse of power, a work of will. We can call his domain "literature" only if we understand that by "literature" he means any writing with any design upon readers—that means, for Burke, all writing. To take Burke seriously, therefore, requires a searching re-examination of some of our traditional "modernist" values; no wonder that we continually put off our appointment with him.

To demonstrate in an adequate way the several claims that I have made on behalf of Burke in these beginning paragraphs is the task of a project more ambitious than the one I have undertaken here. There is a route into Burke, however, that will at least afford us a number of rapid views of subjects he has opened up with his usual provocation. I am referring to his repeated turning to ideas of history and his practice as a reader of history. Burke keeps coming back both to philosophical speculation on the nature of history and to the writing and doing of the historical discipline—these are not separate intellectual activities, as Hayden White has argued, and Burke is good evidence for White's point of view—as if the confrontation with history, even more than the formulation of what he has called dramatism, were the act that conferred identity upon his career. Dramatism is Burke's official program, the name he has given to his system. *Attitudes Toward History*, the title of his fifth volume, gives us access to what I think is a more fundamental Burkean activity— one that contemporary literary intellectuals have consistently shied away from: a process of formulating, exploring, making forays—in so many words, the various acts of reading and writing history. Though Burke brings off this sort of act with maximum penetration and originality, and though I think it (not dramatism) his more fundamental project, the historical act of thinking in evidence in his texts is not—and cannot by virtue of what he makes it—be systematic. What may define him best as a historical thinker, in fact, is a series of decisive engagements, spread over his entire intellectual development, with the idea of system itself. As we'll see, the desire to be systematic, or formally clean, is met at critical points by a resistance to system and in particular by a resistance to the essentializing consequences of systematizing thought.

1

With the work of Martin Heidegger, his student Hans-Georg Gadamer, and from another quarter, Hayden White, now behind us, we need no longer argue that the starting point for any consideration of "history" (whether as discipline or as referent, the temporal record itself) is necessarily with the act of interpretation and the location of that act within a sociocultural matrix. Burke's major early work belongs to the sociocultural matrix of the late 1920s and 1930s. While *Counter-Statement* (1931), *Permanence and Change* (1935), *Attitudes Toward History* (1937), and *The Philosophy of Literary Form* (1941) can be read as preparation for the huge books on motives (*A Grammar of Motives*, 1945, and *A Rhetoric of Motives*, 1950), they are interesting in their own right, as documents marked by the social and intellectual conflicts of the 1930s. Burke is a man of the 1930s, and when the *Grammar* and the *Rhetoric* are understood as productions of such a man, much of what appears forbiddingly abstract and even arid in those books comes richly to life.

In *Permanence and Change*, his first sustained book on these issues of history and interpretation, Burke's thought is marked by contradictory impulses—first to preserve and cherish human differences in their distinguishing particularities, in their discordance of voice, and therefore to check and resist the homogenizing sweep of history conceived as a unified "story"—whether linear, or cyclical, or dialectical; second, and at the same time, his thought is marked by a desire to move directly to a perch above historical process in an effort to find a single mastering structure, a single meaning for it all. The first impulse, pressed hard enough, can produce no theory of history, if we are to conceive of history as finally some single narrative, producing a dominant if not a monolithic meaning. The first impulse would move so assiduously against this idea of history, so assiduously toward a pluralization of history that it would drain almost all meaning from the term. History, radically enough reconceived as histories, is really the despair of history.[3] The second impulse, pressed hard enough, will not only give us history as a unified narrative—let us say of class struggle, or of Christological process, or of Aryan supremacy—but will also, in its most monstrous manifestation, produce a desire to master so powerful that anything might serve history's will. In its softer, liberal bourgeois and literary phase—we'll see an example of it in Burke shortly—a unified theory of history tends to produce complacency and quietism. Either impulse, however, and this is the point, whether anti- or superhistorical, becomes a mode of reading, of understanding, a way of dealing with the historical process.

Permanence and Change opens with a declaration which to our self-congratulatory retrospection sounds uncannily up to date: "all living things are critics."[4] Burke means that all living things are interpreters, and he goes on to distinguish human interpreters from animals by proposing that human beings alone have the capacity to interpret their own interpretations and to reflect upon the very process of reading and interpretation itself.[5] Further along in the argument, he adds that it is never reality in itself but only and always interpretation of reality that we deal with. He points out that even those things we tend to think possess the most stubbornly natural being—he names stimuli and motives as chief examples—are distinctly linguistic products and, as such, terms *of* and *for* interpretation.[6] Burke would refuse to grant to the interpretive process the reassurances that we feel when we anchor (think we anchor) our various readings to the truth of natural reality's fixed rock. As a prolegomenon to any future hermeneutics, we must investigate the basis of the interpretive act with the knowledge that "reality" cannot be that basis. To this end, at an agonized moment in *Permanence and Change*, he describes the hermeneutic situation as a "Babel of orientations." He asks "what arises as a totality" from this Babel? And he answers: "the reenforcement of the interpretive attitude itself."[7] With no way of making a unified interpretation out of Babel, with no totality ("totalization") possible, Burke would seem to have denied a shared basis for the interpretive process, would seem to have plunged interpretation so deeply into the temporal and cultural differences of human particularity as to have engendered an asocial vision of history as a chaos of interpretive attitudes, of innumerable histories, all private, all inaccessibly locked away within their various prison-houses of language.

But at the end of *Permanence and Change* Burke manages a double escape. By rooting human motivation in an ontological principle of freedom which itself is situated outside the historical process, "prior to any particular historic texture," he establishes a point of view outside history from which to mediate (tame) the conflicting interpretations within it.[8] If in its strict sense of *spatially situated vision*, point of view implies that many "points" are possible, Burke's is no point of view. To indulge in a necessary contradiction, Burke's is the spatially ubiquitous point of view of God—the space of freedom itself—a historically uncoerced and unsituated understanding of the congeries of interpretations that discerns their hidden principle of coherence, what all conflicting interpretations aim at—a shared desire whose object, the full realization of freedom in the stream of actual historical life, may be called "transcendental." Moreover, this thesis of the desire for freedom that is "prior" to history, grounded in human nature itself, assumes "that no given *historical* texture need be accepted as the underlying basis of a universal causal series."[9] This principle of freedom, then, would not only resolve the hermeneutic Babel of history by providing a universal motive for interpretation; at the same time it would prohibit any locally engendered reading of the historical process from establishing priority and power as the key to all history's meaning. So the ontological principle of freedom sanctions Burke's transcendent authority as an interpretive subject because, as the ultimate motor principle of interpretation, the desire that moves all interpretation but is not itself caught up in the conflicts and partialities of interpretation, it is identical with the origin of a history that in itself is an arena of confusion and unfreedom, a narrative process whose futile object is the recovery of freedom for social life.

Burke's response to historical complexity in *Permanence and Change* is world-weary and nostalgic for the purity of a paradise called freedom. This is a side of him that cannot be ignored; in various guises it reappears in each of his major books. This attitude toward history, this radically antinomian impulse will

become in another, political phase of his literary theory a re-
source of great emancipating force directed against all systematizing and centralized efforts to control human beings. Here,
within the context of his theories of history, I call this attitude
"aesthetic" (in the classical sense) because in its response to the
immensely variegated historical world of human motives, it produces not a liberating but an impatient and insecure vision, a
need to master and shape diversity into luminous and predictable pattern by giving it a plot. For Burke, in this early book, the
"story" of history is that of the "fall" into unfreedom. We are
called back to Greek philosophy and a distinction in Aristotle's
Poetics that has structured and biased much of Western thought
on the relations of artistic and historical disciplines: I refer to the
idea that history (both as a kind of writing, a discipline, and as the
untextualized temporal process) is bogged down in intransi-
gent, irrational particularity (to echo Philip Sidney's neo-
Aristotelianism) while art traffics in the realm of the universal.
The history of theories of history tends to show that if you begin
with the assumption that historical process is an unintelligible
chaos you will make it meaningful, you will textualize history
(because you won't be able to tolerate your assumption) in ap-
proximately the way that Aristotle said the poet would make
human reality intelligible: you will constitute historical process in
and through a literary mode. This aestheticizing textualization of
history (in *Metahistory* White claims this process is inevitable) is
also its essentialization.

From the vast and confusing historical panorama of human
motives, one is selected as the essence (self-sufficient ground or
core) of motivation, while all others are done away with as forces
in their own right, by being relegated to the status of variants or
departures from the essence that is single, unitary, infinitely
repeatable, and therefore fundamentally real—in a genealogical
formulation of great moment, Burke calls it the ancestral cause of
all other motives.[10] Against this essentializing strategy of interpretation, which he defines as the normal ideal of science to
explain the complex in terms of the simple, Burke places a "proportional" or "playful" strategy that is at rest with complex
interrelations of motives. Such complexities cannot be reduced;
the interpreter must let them be. These two strategies of interpretation are at work in Burke's books from the beginning. And

though in his two interpretations of interpretation he clearly elevates one over the other, neither such valorization nor the mere fact of high-level hermeneutic self-consciousness permits him to master the essentializing impulse in his writing. I deliberately echo in this paragraph the language of Derrida's influential essay "Structure, Sign, and Play in the Discourse of the Human Sciences," not to lay his ideas over Burke's but to indicate two things. First, the rather complete anticipation of a major Derridean point of view in Burke's essay on Freud of 1939; second, to emphasize in Burke's work a point easily missed, and too often ignored in Derrida's well-known essay: that there is never a question of choosing between these strategies. No single interpretive subject is free to work its will in the hermeneutic process because the subject cannot master the forces at work *in* reading and *on* the reader.

The relocation of the interpreter of history, as traditional Cartesian subject, from its place of mastery and freedom to a function of a process of history larger and more powerful than itself has crucial consequences in Burke's later writings. At this point, however, and in somewhat artificial fashion, I want to segregate his essentializing impulse in order to examine its implications in greater detail. In *Attitudes Toward History* Burke offers two interpretive keys to history. The basic historical process he calls, in a phrase of considerable wit, "the bureaucratization of the imaginative"; the central interpretive attitude that he will take toward this process, his attitude of attitudes toward history, is the comic one. [11] But let us not take his distinctions at face value, for what is signified by the phrase "bureaucratization of the imaginative" is not (Burke's philosophical principles would never permit it to be) the reality in itself of history's process but an interpretation of it, and the comic attitude is a perfectly complementary way of responding to (living with) such a reading of history. The comic response turns out to be a consoling and accommodating interpretation of interpretation.

After opening his definition of the "bureaucratization of the imaginative" by calling it "a basic process of history," Burke quickly reveals the utopian, pastoral, and origin-oriented bias of his position: "Perhaps it merely names the process of dying. 'Bureaucratization' is an unwieldy word, perhaps even an onomatopoeia, since it sounds as bungling as the situation it would characterize. 'Imaginative' suggests pliancy, liquidity, the vernal. And with it we couple the incongruously bulky and almost unpronounceable."[12] With an aesthete's vengeance, Burke sets up a critique of the everyday life of the historical process as the Calibanization of Ariel—or is it that what he bemoans is not so much the historical process at large as the coming to being of repressive social organizations within an industrial setting and the various hegemonic instruments that keep them in place? He continues:

> Gide has said somewhere that he distrusts the carrying-out of one possibility because it necessarily restricts other possibilities. Call the possibilities "imaginative." And call the carrying-out of one possibility the *bureaucratization* of the imaginative. An imaginative possibility (usually at the start Utopian) is bureaucratized when it is embodied in the realities of a social texture, in all the complexities of language and habits, in the property relationships, the methods of government, production and distribution, and in the development of rituals that re-enforce the same emphasis. It follows that in this "imperfect world," no imaginative possibility can ever attain complete bureaucratization . . . . In bureaucratizing a possibility, we necessarily come upon the necessity of compromise, since human beings are not a perfect fit for *any* historic texture.[13]

With this thinly veiled scorn for any and all sociohistoric textures that have been, are, and will be, with this concomitant idealistic projection of human being as a precariously fortified essence that can only be soiled, distorted, and encumbered by all actual and possible modes of government, production, and property relations, and with this keen perception of what Antonio Gramsci called hegemony, Burke has given us a portrait of historical life as an arena of constriction with no exit. "Hegemony": sophisticated political "rule" that transforms an openly coercive, bullying "domination" into "consent," even into a form of "self-governance"; at its politically clever best, in its most mature form, in the United States, an educative strategy of ruling interests to defuse recalcitrant and rebellious subjects, to extend and perpetuate their domination by saturating the whole process of living, our sense of ourselves, our relations, our lived world, with their values, with no need to coerce through physical force; the "development of rituals that reinforce the same emphasis." Tragically, all hope is situated at the freshness of origins, where (and when) imagination freely creates and plays with its possibilities of utopian vision: all subsequent historical movement away from the playful and contemplative consideration of multiple visions and into action—into the *act*ualization of vision—is synonymous with a process of degradation, of the loss of freedom, even of dying. No telos is discernible as an end to history's futility because historical process is not purposive.

But Burke's key reading of the bureaucratization of the imaginative is precisely not tragic. If tragedy implies necessarily dangerous limitations upon our capacity to know, and if an inescapable consequence of these limitations is that we act accordingly—self-destructively, in partial darkness, never able to free ourselves from the fatal mesh of circumstance—then Burke has appropriately named his attitude toward history "comic," for it postulates not fatal ignorance and death but foolishness and embarrassing exposure for the human agent, as well as full consciousness for what I must call the comedic master of the twists and turns of the human drama, a confident and complete knowledge of how the game begins and how it will end. Burke is that comedic master who would teach us the lessons of humility. With the security of his knowledge that history inevitably bungles imaginative possibility, that with amusing (because mechanical) repetition the insight of imagination will always, because it is materially embodied, turn on its bureaucratizing agents, and that historical action necessarily ends in gaping discrepancies between intention and actualization, Burke himself becomes the exemplary humble man, no champion of a single program because he knows in advance how all programs will turn out. History is thus essentialized in the mode of dramatic irony, with a privileged place given to the man of comedic knowledge who, though he must be foolish actor, is somehow wise spectator as well. As comedic master Burke becomes what he exhorts others to be—an observer of himself while acting, an achiever of *"maximum consciousness"* who can "'transcend' himself by noting his own foibles."[14] How more openly can we aestheticize history than by constituting it through the lens of a literary category? How more openly can we essentialize history than by squeezing it all under the umbrella of a single genre? To jam history into the narrow room of a single comedic plot, as Burke has done, is surely to press in most aggressive fashion Aristotle's claim for the poet's universalizing power, while, as a consequence, such single-minded narrative conversion of historical process wipes out the differences of historical textures and moves in another way against that threatening Babel of interpretation that Burke had repressed in *Permanence and Change.*

Though neither the older nor the newer generation of Yale New Critics has shown much overt speculative or practical concern for history, some such essentializing attitude as Burke's underwrites their respective formalist projects for literary study, with paradox, wit, and irony at work in the essays of Cleanth Brooks to essentialize literary history (collapsing Wordsworth into Donne), and with *différance*, aporia, and undecidability similarly at work in de Man's writing to elide differences among Rousseau, Nietzsche, and Yeats. In both generations of Yale critics what is assumed is a highly synchronized, idealistic sense of literary-historical process rooted in a principle of deep continuity. As Wimsatt put it in the introduction to the critical history he wrote with Brooks, all theories are "engaged with a common reality . . . . Literary problems occur not just because history produces them, but because literature is a thing of such and such a sort. . . ."[15] Wimsatt's carefully turned phrasing, which respects literature's complex and more than literary involvement ("not just because") is obliterated in the purer formalisms of his Yale successors. His feeling for intelligible and persistent literary substance becomes the ground for strong historical coherence—and it tends to go with a sensibility disposed to comedy (Wimsatt and de Man may be joined at this point, despite their different interpretations of what that substance is). The recent essays of de Man are wonderful epitomes of comic vision, and his key terms provide verification. His criticism of difference ends by affirming what the comedic master has always known—that in the end all human differences make no difference because all historical ("bureaucratizing") forces of differentiation are simply "torn apart" (de Man's words) by a power that returns literature to radical freedom from all context, except its own literary-historical context, just as Prospero, in the end, permits Ariel's return to unfettered airiness.[16] De Man's earlier criticism of allegory and irony demonstrates that true comic mastery lies in the acute self-consciousness of the fall even as we fall—falling being inevitable. And in his celebrated work of the 1970s, there is repeated stress on the necessary ironic interdependence, in literary criticism of the highest order, of programmatic "blindness" with intuitive (imaginative) "insight." De Man attempts to demonstrate the ensnarement of critical theorists themselves in a comedic identity: thus "theory" joins "literature" in a fatalistic vision of history as the recurrence of a primal scene—man the self-conscious bungler, eternally bound to the wheel, laughing knowingly all the way, and, best comedic sign of all in de Man's thought, somehow succeeding (this is de Man's happy ending), producing insight in spite of himself.

The linkage of the persistent formalist projects of Brooks and de Man, whose work stretches from the 1930s to the 1980s, with Burke's comic meditation on history might remind us of what we are likely to forget in our zeal to banish formalism in the name of a "responsible" scholarship of historical life: that the comedic formalism of Burke was born in the 1930s, in the midst of the worst socioeconomic crisis this country has known. Comedic formalism may be denigrated as romantic escapism, but it is nevertheless one kind of response to crisis, and certainly it is one kind of alternative to the aesthetic of social realism that Burke, Brooks, and de Man saw, especially in the earlier phases of their careers, as a major threat to the understanding of literary discourse. The inaugural step of any modern formalism constitutes a double negation: on the one hand, of naive theories of social realism, and, on the other, of the philosophical support of such theories in a vulgar version of Marxism. (To be a man of the 1930s, as I have called Burke, is not necessarily to be a man of the left, though I think in a sophisticated way he is that too.) The formalisms of Burke, Brooks, and de Man have a social context, and they promise for the contemporary literary mind, in the wisdom of their comedic sense of history, what another comedy—*commedia*—promised for the medieval theological imagination: a paradise, this one secular and literary, in which the fruit of transcendence is not the end of history but a maximum knowledge of what (literary) history is, has been, and will be, from a vantage point beyond its conflicts: the critic as comedic master takes the place of God. The self-consciousness of Burke's and de Man's comedic master is the one space of freedom within the prison of history.

What the comedic historian knows, what he takes to be the single truth of history is that there is no truth, but only fools of truth. Burke wrote the following, but de Man might have:

The progress of humane enlightenment can go no further than in picturing people not as *vicious*, but as *mistaken*. When you add that people are *necessarily* mistaken, that all people are exposed to situations in which they must act as fools, that *every* insight contains its own special kind of blindness, you complete the comic circle, returning again to the lesson of humility that underlies great tragedy. The audience, from its vantage point, sees the operation of errors that the characters of the play cannot see; thus seeing two angles at once, it is chastened by dramatic irony; it is admonished to remember that when intelligence means *wisdom* . . . it requires fear, resignation, the sense of limits, as an important ingredient.[17]

We need to distinguish this Burkean theory of comedy from its classical forefathers. Whereas Aristotle and numerous of his Renaissance progeny relegated to comedy the representation of man as worse than he is—more frail, more prone to error, with the implication that such representation (derived really from a judgment upon lower, politically marginal classes) is a deviation from a norm of human behavior—Burke at this point joins with other modernists and pushes the comedic deviation to normative status by declaring in effect that comedy is the representation of man as he really is. The Burkean comedic vision encapsulates truth in a metaphysics of foolishness and failure. This comedic knowledge—this ultimate of "humane enlightenment" that is the repeated message of modernist literary theory from Brooks to de Man—this ironic vision that declares the inability of literature to declare, refer, or have a message, would call all injunctions to act at best naiveté, at worst fanaticism; this so-called humane enlightenment (which masks a dread of powerlessness) would, in its "wise" counsel of "resignation" and "fear," uphold the status quo. The criticisms of comedy, paradox, irony, aporia, and *différance*, far from being socially innocent, or socially indifferent, sum up for many liberal humanist intellectuals, particularly those with memories of the 1930s, a certain attitude, a social posture, and a philosophy of history that now passes, especially in literary-critical academe, for sophisticated worldliness; it is in the end a mandarin coolness that betrays itself in the bewildering variety of ways that it has found in which to declare *noli me tangere*, for I belong to despair. Or is it, as Gramsci suggests, the defensive posture of an active will that fears its position is weak? Since both tragedy and comedy are the major literary forms that promote, in Burke's terms, attitudes of social acceptance and accomodation, the quietism of literary politics is almost a foregone conclusion.[18]

Within the history of theories of comedy, then, there is inscribed another history. The history of theories of comedy is itself a literary sign of that major shift in social history marked by the rise of bourgeois power. Originally theorized by Aristotle within the highly stratified class structure of his slave-holding society as a representation of "lower" or "meaner" types, comedy bears for him a social and political vision, not a moral one (as in any number of Christianized Renaissance neo-Aristotelians). The literary difference between tragedy and comedy in Aristotle is the production of a social difference and the highly active political repression that undergirds social difference. For Burke, genuine American original of middle class origins, the translation of comedic vision into an anthropological generalization about "all people" is a different form of sociological projection—the affirmation of bourgeois class values as universal, the mark of horizontal or democratic political desire. In Burke's American perspective, comedy, not tragedy, becomes the privileged literary mode—the articulation, at once, of bourgeois political ideals and of a conception of human nature that highlights this crippling contradiction: the "free" and "universal" bourgeois subject finds the highest wisdom to be a fatalistic, detached observation of a hardened, closed system in which one inevitably fails, a world he never made and whose laws he cannot alter.

2

With this "comedic" approach to a theory of "maximum consciousness" in *Attitudes Toward History*, Burke is prepared to stake out his most essentialist program in the introduction to *A Grammar of Motives*—what he calls dramatism but what we would now, with hindsight, call structuralism. The *Grammar* of 1945 is full-blown structuralism well in advance of the French structuralist movement. More interesting even than his anticipation of Lévi-Strauss and company is the way Burke, in several keenly self-conscious moments in his book, forecasts the critique of structuralism mounted in the work of Foucault and Derrida. In less systematic form Burke's involvement with a structuralist method dates from the title essay of *The Philosophy of Literary Form*: it is concretely in evidence in his exemplary analysis of the binary coordinates of Clifford Odets's play *Golden Boy*, which is shown to be the expression of a binary code, a productive mechanism, or model of antithetical values behind the actual discourse of the play; at a certain level of analysis, this binary code is even said to be an expression of the "psychic economy" of Odets's mind—an economy that is in turn expressive of a larger cultural economy.[19] In theoretical terms Burke's structuralism surfaces in *The Philosophy of Literary Form* when, in an attempt to claim an ur-form for drama, he argues that he is making no genetic, historical, or empirical claim: "We are proposing it as a *calculus*—a vocabulary, or set of coordinates that serves best for the integration of all phenomena studied by the social sciences."[20] A few sentences later he drops a footnote to the discussion in which he explains that he is at work on a book—it will be called *A Grammar of Motives*—where the study of motivation will be identical with the *"structure"* of texts and that, further, structure in all kinds of texts— philosophical, theological, fictional, juridical, scientific, and so on—can be accounted for by five key terms which, in their hierarchically disposed interrelations and their subtle play, can be thought of as exhausting the structural possibilities of textual expression.[21] Still a little further on in the same general discussion, and in another footnote, Burke subtly qualifies this voracious synchronic totalization of history by introducing diachrony, difference, and dialectic into the system in such a way that the systemic power of his five key terms (act, scene, agent, agency, purpose) is prohibited from accounting for change before change in fact occurs.[22] Again with hindsight, we can say that *A Grammar of Motives* is generated, at least in what I would think most contemporary critical theorists should find its most significant sections, by a conflict of hermeneutical impulses—call them synchrony and diachrony. And again, as both Burke and

Derrida would remind us, there is never any question of choosing between them, never any question of segregating them as if the interpreting subject (Burke, Derrida, or anyone else) could master the process of reading.

Burke introduces his dramatistic version of structuralism ("dramatistic" because his five key terms are derived from an analysis of drama) via a Kantian essentialism of mind that he converts into a plan for something like a "critique of pure motives": "The book is concerned with the basic forms of thought which, in accordance with the nature of the world as all men necessarily experience it, are exemplified in the attributing of motives."[23] Then very quickly he textualizes Kant's epistemological idealism by removing the "forms of thought" from their traditional Kantian intersubjective location to their contemporary home within intertextual space: "These forms of thought . . . are equally present in systematically elaborated metaphysical structures, in legal judgments, in poetry and fiction, in political and scientific works, in news and in bits of gossip offered at random."[24] This textualization of Kant is not quite enough in itself, however, to save Burke from the idealistic reduction of history at work in some of the theoretical sections of his earlier books. For when he speaks of this textualization, he speaks of the forms of thought "embodied" in discourse—a term that would place ultimate value not on discursive practice but on the subjective and prediscursive origins of some *dis*embodied geometry of mind.[25] In this same vein, he recalls for us his preoccupation with the "bureaucratization of the imaginative" when he refers to his grammatical resources as "principles" and the various philosophies that apply these principles as "*casuistries*" which seek to insert principles, by definition ahistorical, into "temporal situations."[26] We are not surprised when Burke indicates in this introduction that he began his *Grammar* not with the notion of writing what in fact turned out, but with the intention of developing a theory of comedy as a way of investigating human relations.

The statement of intention in the *Grammar* is structuralist through and through and a summation of where he has been as a thinker since *Counter-Statement*: "We want to inquire into the purely internal relationships which the five terms bear to one another, considering their possibilities of transformation, their range of permutations and combinations—and then to see how these various resources figure in the actual statements about human motives. Strictly speaking we mean by a Grammar of motives a concern with the terms alone, without reference to the ways in which their potentialities have been or can be utilized in actual statements about motives."[27] This intention to concern himself with the internal legality of terminological rules that governs globally the production of texts constitutes the classical austerity of the structuralist ideal. By the end of his introduction, Burke has indulged the cold-blooded Platonism of the most extreme kind of structuralism when, with uncharacteristic contempt for cultural and historical differences and particularities and changes, he violently synchronizes the historical process, as he had done earlier in *Permanence and Change*, with this claim: "Our work must be synoptic . . . in the sense that it offers a system of placement, and should enable us, by the systematic manipulation of the terms, to 'generate,' or 'anticipate' the various classes of motivational theory."[28]

Kenneth Burke never played the role of the pseudo-scientific structuralist god very well; other passages in the introduction to the *Grammar* and numerous places in the body of the text show that his heart was some place else. As a synchronist Burke must necessarily endow his five key terms with a solidity massive enough to withstand diachronic pressure. Yet even in the process of formulating his high-flying Platonic structuralism, Burke introduces theoretical qualifications that open up his method to a level of historical analysis generally untouched by structuralists. In *The Philosophy of Literary Form* he distinguishes "between positive and dialectical terms—the former being terms that do not require an opposite to define, the latter being terms that do require an opposite."[29] The distinction between positive and dialectical is not quite the distinction of Saussure's linguistics between "substantialist" and "differential" terms: "dialectical" sometimes implies a difference of a very special sort, a difference that eventually may not evade the metaphysics of a "positive" or "substantialist" vocabulary. Nevertheless, the general intention of his distinction is clear and valuable. With it we move from a realm of natural, fixed, or eternalized meaning to the human arena where meaning is made and unmade, enforced and subverted, assented to and resisted in collective acts of will, where nothing (or very little) is natural, fixed, and eternal. The further toward dialectical or differential status Burke can manage to move his key terms and the temporally frozen model they imply, the closer he engages the inherent synchrony of his grammatical project with a fluid diachrony of historical process.

But that is not quite a fair way to put the issue, insofar as I have implied that synchrony has nothing to do with history and that diachrony and "true" history are to be identified. The joining of synchrony and diachrony vastly complicates Burke's idea of history and thereby opens for analysis a historical reality that preserves the long endurance of a synchronic totality, the immense staying-power of certain deeply rooted habits of sense-making— we can call this activity in history "tradition" or "tradition-making"—and at the same time preserves forces of change internal to the totality (that untotalize, unsynchronize it), forces that provide a certain complexity within a system that is (this is one meaning of "system") inherently simplifying. These forces (histories within history) thicken and make heterogeneous historical textures that tradition and system would homogenize. Like interpretation, history is never synchrony or diachrony, never essential or proportional ("playful"). It is both. Some time in the late 1930s and early 1940s Burke developed theories of interpretation that began to do justice to his practice as a reader of history's texts.

As he puts it in his very complicated introduction to the *Grammar*, "what we want is *not terms that avoid ambiguity*, but *terms that clearly reveal the strategic spots at which ambiguities necessarily arise*."[30] The important words here, I think, are "ambiguity," "strategic," and "necessarily." Apparently the terms that Burke seeks do not merely reveal ambiguity, themselves free of it in their essentialist heaven: the terms themselves produce ambiguity, they are the *"resources"* of ambiguity, to use Burke's word, and because they are the resources of ambiguity they are ultimately—as terminological grandfathers—producers of what ambiguity itself produces, "transformation": "it is in the areas of ambiguity that transformations take place; in fact, without such areas, transformation would be impossible."[31] Burke is giving us here, both as theory of interpretation and theory of history, not the comfortable view of the structuralist lineage of sense-making, with principles of sense-making themselves outside the structural fields of history, or the equally comfortable view of recent

Yale critics. The latter group tends to force "undecidability" to function allegorically as an instrument that cancels out all conflicts of force in order to create one recurrent thematic conflict, which then becomes the sign of what is called "textuality" (the "literary"), a principle, in de Man's work, of fatality and essentialization in the domain of literary history. When Burke defines his project as that of studying and clarifying the resources of ambiguity, for the end of illuminating moments of transformation, he is proposing a genealogical approach to history that would situate itself outside the perspectives of our dominant critical models.

If it is helpful to have a term for what Burke does best as a reader of history, the term "critical structuralist" might be fair. And since one of my purposes all along has been to argue his uncanny contemporaneity, "critical structuralist" is doubly useful to me, for it indicates not only his anticipation of structuralism but also its most recent critique. The crucial strategy in the service of this critical structuralism is Burke's ruthless investigation of his own terminological resources. The deep bias of his dramatistic system is unavoidably humanistic because the very notion of dramatism rests on the distinction between "action" (a uniquely human movement) and "motion" (a process that presumably characterizes all nonhuman movement). At face value his five key terms (act, scene, agent, agency, purpose) are unarguably humanistic. It can be no accident that when Burke lists his terms, it is always in that order, with "act" leading off. And his formulation of what he calls master ratios (act-scene, agent-scene) only reinforces the humanism of the system. Yet the liberal humanist privilege granted to the autonomous actor-subject (with its corollary values of freedom, creativity, self-possession, and self-presence) is probably the primary focus of Burke's critical consciousness. He performs about as thorough an act of what is now called "deconstruction" as is possible, but when he is finished he has not destroyed the humanistic impulse of his dramatism; he has only (and this by design) relocated the "free" subject within a system that is now understood in more complex fashion than his usual bare-bones formulation of dramatism would permit. Let me put that point in another way: the humanist conception of "agent" is understood in the widest context—it is seen as *having* a constraining context, which is precisely what humanism has difficulty admitting. But such understanding (that the subject is a function of a system) cannot and should not eliminate all humanist desire for the free subject—a point that many recent antihumanists are not yet ready to concede.

Burke's critique of what would be called structuralism is really a critique of systematic thought itself, including his own. A major portion of *A Grammar of Motives* is devoted to an investigation of the systematic dimension of the various schools in the history of philosophy. More specifically, Burke wants to show how each of the philosophical schools derives its distinctive character from the peculiar genius of an "ancestral term."[32] Though all of the classical systems find a significant role for each of the five terms to play, the identity of any given system will be generated by an ancestral term, and this term, to stay with Burke's metaphor, in effect fathers all the rest because they are conceived, not independently, as having terminological lives and rights of their own, but only in relation to the father: *their* identity is simply flooded by father-influence. Systems, then, are essentialized by their ancestral terms, and it is one of Burke's strongest insights to point out that essentialization is the product of a genealogical will to power. By probing the notion of "ancestral term," Burke uncovers the secret power of systematic thinking and the essentializing thrust of his own system.

Moving critically against the terms "act" and "agent" he goes directly for the jugular of dramatism. This criticism of act and agent—it will recall, before him, certain passages in Nietzsche's *The Will to Power* and, after him, Derrida and de Man—not only deliberately sets off an undermining effect throughout the *Grammar*: it retrospectively revises Burke's attitudes toward those quintessentially actional terms "freedom" (in *Permanence and Change*) and "imagination" (in *Attitudes Toward History*). For an act to be itself and not a disguised term for scene, Burke says (de Man later echoes this in his essay "Literary History and Literary Modernity") that it must possess a wholly arbitrary (magical) dimension; the act that is truly an act presumes creativity in the literal sense.[33] No act is truly an act, then, unless it can be shown to have a radically originating function. No matter how assiduously secular the philosophical systems which feature it, all ideas of act will be traced to some sort of theological conception: "God would thus be perfect action," and of course perfect agent, "in that there would be no motivating principle beyond his own nature."[34] The self-irony running throughout Burke's discussion of act is that for an act to be truly itself it cannot be permitted to have a place within a system of other terms—it must, like God himself, stand in a perfect purity of isolation.

Now, if Burke's analysis of act reveals that the most secular and liberal-minded celebration of the human subject as autonomous source of action and value rests on theological support, what about his own featuring of act? Let us recall that he inaugurates the system with a distinction between action and motion and that he situates act and agent within a network of five terms. Does act or agent essentialize Burkean dramatism? Are his five key terms thinly masked versions of an ancestral term? Is he, after all, a traditional humanist? Or is it the peculiar virtue of his system to subvert the essentializing power of even his own ancestral terms? Burke answers our questions—not really ours, since it is his text that provides us with such ammunition. What I am about to quote from *A Grammar of Motives* is in the strict sense a deconstruction of the subject-agent:

> We may discern a dramatistic pun, involving a merger of active and passive in the expression, "the motivation of an act." Strictly speaking, the act of an agent would be the movement not of one *moved* but of a mover (a mover of the self or of something else by the self). For an act is by definition active, whereas to be moved (or motivated) is by definition passive. Thus, if we quizzically scrutinize the expression, "the motivating of an act," we note that it implicitly contains the paradox of substance. Grammatically, if a construction is active, it is not passive; and if it is passive, it is not active. But to consider an *act* in terms of its *grounds* is to consider it in terms of what it is not, namely, in terms of motives that, in acting upon the active, would make it passive. We could state the paradox another way by saying that the concept of activation implies a kind of passive-behind-the-passive; for an agent who is "motivated by his passions" would be "moved by his being-movedness" or "acted upon by his state of being acted upon."[35]

Burke's unhinging of the traditional conception of the subject and its central category of a consciousness whose *active* power is coincidental with itself, entirely in control of itself, lucid, and self-present, is rooted in what he discovers to be the radical duplicity of the very cornerstone terms of Western philosophical discourse. What he has done to "act" (another foreshadowing, with a difference, of de Man) could be extended to agent, agency, purpose, and scene and, more importantly even than those words, to the word of words for any mode of thought, philosophical or otherwise, that would consider itself disciplined. I am referring to Burke's glancing reference to the "paradox of substance." "Substance": a term indispensible not only to all manner of metaphysical thinking but also (and perhaps this is a way of gauging the impulse to metaphysics in us all) in every attempt to *define*—something, anything at all, in every attempt, in other words, to be intellectually rigorous, precise, and above all serious.

In his stunning discussion of the "paradox of substance," Burke locates in the term a strange self-difference. Substance differs from itself, for it moves between a sense that denotes what a thing intrinsically is—that part of the thing uniquely there and nowhere else, that makes the thing what it is and confers its special identity—and a sense (etymologically evident) that denotes a thing's support: *sub-stance*, that upon which the thing stands, what is beneath it—its "foundation" (from the Greek: a standing under). The paradox, then, is that "the word 'substance,' used to designate what a thing *is*, derives from a word designating what a thing is *not*. That is, though used to designate something *within* the thing, intrinsic to it, the word etymologically refers to something *outside* the thing, *extrinsic* to it."[36] Or, to sharpen the paradox still further: used ordinarily to refer to the special interior presence of a thing, etymologically the word refers us to a context, again "something that the thing is *not*."[37] In this strategic terminological moment, when the "intrinsic and extrinsic change places," we confront the bedrock of the "antinomy of definition."[38] It is a perilous kind of bedrock, however, since no secure footing is provided; it is precisely security, in fact, that Burke is doing away with. The concept of substance, the one thing that must not differ from itself if definition is to be definition, is endowed with what Burke calls an "unresolvable ambiguity," but which we can call, after Derrida, "undecidability," since no choice can be made between two very different senses.[39] This perverse playfulness of undecidability, in evidence in

Burke's cultivation of the paradoxes of substance and act, is not the despair of history. Rather, it is first the very condition of transformation that makes a certain kind of historical consciousness possible; second, it is the condition that opens, once and for all, the autonomous, closed, and unified subject to historical process; Burke deconstructs the subject *in order to* historicize it; and third, by questioning and subverting the fundamental "originating" claim of "action," Burke's dramatistic dance on "action" radically historicizes its significance. With the self-presence of key Western terms like "substance" and "act" so unstabilized by Burke's analysis, we are prepared to confront, in the terminological dimension itself, a more detailed and heterogeneous level of history than we have been accustomed to knowing.

3

Burke's interest in his *Grammar* in philosophical history is focused on the power of systematic thought to reproduce and extend itself while at the same time engendering internal fissures and conflicts—and in general the very possibility of the transformation of modes of thought that tend to resist transformation. This kind of interest in the history of philosophy is not for its own sake; the history of philosophy for Burke is part of a larger historical process; and the analysis of philosophical discourse is meant to be exemplary, a way into that process. To this point I have been concerned with exposing the theoretical bases of the act of interpretation in Burke, rather than with his analysis of any concrete historical texture. I turn only now to his practice, not because theory is a higher thing and must come first but because I don't think his readings can be appreciated in their wider implications unless their theoretical qualities are grasped: his theories of reading imply a historical process of a particular sort.

The closer we move in Burke toward the analysis of specific historical textures, especially of the political sort, the more we need the concept provocatively put forth by Gramsci in his *Prison Notebooks*; I refer again to the concept of "hegemony," Gramsci's great revision of Marxist dialogue on the relations of an economic base to superstructural expressions of culture: hegemony as a Marxist account of the decentered subject.[40] Though he could not have known Gramsci's writings until most of his own books had long been written, Burke's dialogue with Marx has been persistent—and remarkably close to Gramsci's revision of the vulgarities of economism. Hegemony in Gramsci, and its counterpart in Burke—he gave it no name—is fundamentally a process of education carried on through various institutions of civil society in order to make normative, inevitable, even "natural" the ruling ideas of ruling interests. The hegemonic process is a way of gaining "free" assent, productivity, and cooperation within a ruling political structure without recourse to violence (the domination of bodies through the means of the military and the police). Hegemonic rule is therefore the mark of the stable, "mature" society whose ideological apparatus is so deeply set in place, so well buried, so unexamined a basis of our judgment and feeling that it is taken for truth with a capital letter. Because the process of rule is an educative one, involving techniques of psychological manipulation on behalf of ruling economic interests, its theory represents a certain union of Marx and Freud, of materialist and psychoanalytic views of history. The ground of Freudo-Marxism is a common one for Burke and Gramsci. If Burke as the comedic historian, or even as the programmatic theorist of parts of the *Grammar*, is a dispassionate observer of historical inevitability and therefore an implicit affirmer of the status quo, then the critical structuralist and student of hegemony is an implicit interventionist who teaches not comedic lessons of humble passiveness but the muscular exercise of a collective will for the ends of social change.

Gramsci's theory of hegemony has its parallel in Burke's idea of an educative process that, largely silent and working mainly at subterranean levels, "moves" us to assent to the structure of property relations authorized by "rules, courts, parliaments, laws, educators, constabulary, and the moral slogans linked with each."[41] These various constituents of ruling interests, especially what Gramsci would call their "traditional intellectuals," and what Burke calls the various "priests"[42] of the pulpit, schools, press, radio, popular arts, (and we add television), educate the socially dispossessed person to feel "that he 'has a stake in' the authoritative structure that dispossesses him; for the influence exerted upon the policies of education by the authoritative structure encourages the dispossessed to feel that his only hope of repossession lies in his allegiance to the structure that had dispossessed him."[43] The dispossessed give their hopes to the dispossessing structure because they have been hegemonically educated to believe that there is no other, no alternative, no better structure.

For Burke, by the late 1930s, the significance of "economics and psychology" was wholly translated by the names "Marx" and "Freud," and the task that he set himself (he claimed it as the informing intention of *Attitudes Toward History*) was to link these names in indissoluble relation.[44] What he had discovered in the late 1930s the Freudian New Left would discover again in the 1960s—that the ground of an integrated theory of society and social change lay in the analysis of the sites and symbols of authority and that, furthermore, it was necessary not to view the family as Christopher Lasch would view it, as haven in a heartless world but, rather, as a mediating link between, on one side, the mode of production and its political levels of expression and reinforcement, and, on the other, the intimate, interior, and apparently nonmaterial region of psychological identity. Burke's symbols of authority bridge (before Fredric Jameson's Lacanian essays) the interior-exterior, subject-object opposition commonly employed to segregate psychology and economics. Psychological and economic spaces overlap. The powerful figures of identity-formation—such figures as parents, doctors, nurses in the so-called prepolitical period of childhood, and such figures, in later life, as foreman or employer—are vehicles of the hegemonic constitution of consciousness that is carried out more overtly in the educative, legislative, and constabulary levels of the political superstructure through its symbolic authorities and representatives.

Alienation, Burke insists, is therefore a psycho-economic concept, synonymous with a need to reject reigning symbols of authority and the property structure undergirding them all.[45] But rejection and, to come directly to the point, rupture and revolution are for Burke the most difficult of attitudes and programs to sustain and carry through in a political practice. Our identities are very nearly hopelessly complicated (beyond self-conscious control) by a hegemonic process that would enroll us in a range of corporate identities, some concentric, others in conflict. The result of such complicating and proliferating coordinations and corporations of identity is to clog and solidify identity to the point where change of the radical sort is almost unimaginable.

Now if we move from personal identity in its social frame, to the frame of the society's identity itself, if we move to a larger historical perspective by adding, as Burke does, that a sociopolitical structure of authority and the hegemonic process proper to it, and which keeps it in force, have astonishing stamina to dominate history over the longest duration, then it would seem to follow that visionary social programs, with their desire for radical rupture in the movement of history, a desire to make it new in the literal sense, can only be frustrated. For such desire (here Burke comes very close to de Man) has for its object the formation of an identity that would imply, in order to be achieved, the destruction of all genealogy, an obliteration of one's entire lineage, a symbolic suicide that involves a symbolic parricide.[46] Burke is speaking of the personal desire for rebirth, but his analysis holds equally well for collective social desire to be reborn in a revolution that would destroy the historical lineage of every society's collective past. Perhaps his most complete example of how hegemonic process works politically is his examination in *Attitudes Toward History* of the "medieval synthesis," the way Thomist philosophy as a mode of intellectual action was a thorough reinforcement and a technique of maintenance of established property relationships in the feudal mode.[47] Burke's exploration of what he calls the "morphological" parallels of Thomism and capitalism is ingenious and compelling, and it foreshadows Foucault's morphological connection of the practice of asceticism with that of the disciplinary society. Burke's analysis is a genealogical reexamination of some of modern Western society's key categories. At this point his synchronist vision, like Foucault's, is sobering, even depressing. Morphologically, he would have us understand that "providence"

> became "investment for profit"; the processes of "justification" took the simple form of "advertising," "salesmanship," and "success"; the close relationship between morality and utility came to a head in the "gospel of service"; the devices of perfidy were exposed in the legal manipulations of contract;

the synthesizing tendencies of man were manifest, as they could never be by experiments with decerebrated frogs, in the growth of holding companies; corporate identity itself was shorn of its unwieldy mysticism when the member of the church, as the "body of Christ," became simply the holder of non-voting stock.[48]

Yet Burke's lesson, easily missed with his stress on the marathon character of historical repression, is not de Man's: the lesson is that radical rupture, not progressive change, is impossible. The shifting forces of hegemonic authority that he traces in the curve of history from ancient Greece through "periods" of Christian evangelism, medieval synthesis, Protestant transition, naive capitalism, and emergent collectivism, while massive and ominously persistent, are not monolithic. Like the terminological keystones of Western philosophical tradition, the dominant sociopolitical structures of the West, despite their totalizing desire to saturate every corner of history, are internally divided, different from themselves in their very "substance." One of Burke's ways of pinpointing structural instability in the tradition (Nicos Poulantzas would make a similar point)[49] is to declare that every so-called historical period is transitional; no period is there, in full presence—historical texture is ineluctably heterogeneous because every social formation is marked by a temporal fissure constituted by the simultaneous "presence" of traces of older, residual modes of production with anticipation of an emergent, critical mode working to establish authority.[50] Another sign of structural instability is that, unlike real estate, the language of privilege and authority is not the private property of any person or class. The linguistic symbols of authority, like "rights" and "freedom," are appropriable—they can be seized by a collective and turned against those who last appropriated them in order to dispossess yet earlier appropriators. This oscillation of rights depends, of course, on the oscillation of power between possessors and dispossessed; the locus of power/rights is never fixed because the locus is not natural. This process, described by Burke as the "stealing back and forth of symbols," is the beginning of any hegemonic education and rule.[51] The point is clear: no hegemonic condition is fatally fixed because no hegemonic condition rests on natural or God-given authority, though it is one of the key strategies of hegemonic education to inculcate those very claims. Like the term "substance," and its paradox of intrinsic and extrinsic, the term "rights" is undecidable, though in this instance the "inside" and the "outside" are not ontological but social terms, better given as the "ins" and the "outs." It is precisely the radical instability (appropriability) of terms like "rights" or "the people" that makes for transformation in philosophical and social history, the historical moment that we can define, with Foucault's help, as an "event," when ruling discourse is seized and, in the name of ruling discourse, turned against the rulers.[52] Burke had already made Foucault's point in his address to the American Writers' Congress in 1935. Here he makes it again in *Attitudes Toward History·*

> The divine right of kings was first invoked by secular interests combating the authority of the theocrats. It held that God appointed the king, rather than the church authorities, to represent the secular interests of "the people." Later, when the church made peace with established monarchs, identifying its interests with the interests of the secular authorities, the church adopted the doctrine as its own. And subsequently the bourgeoisie repudiated the doctrine, in repudiating both monarch and state. It did so in the name of "rights," as the doctrine had originally been promulgated in the name of "rights." Among these "rights" was "freedom." And Marx in turn stole this bourgeois symbol for the proletariat.[53]

In another (Nietzschean) meditation on the same phenomenon of the passage (genealogy) of "rights," this rite of appropriation, which reflects the increasing stress on language as the center of his theory of history, Burke notes that it is precisely the ontological emptiness of the term—it is always differentially, or dialectically, or contextually defined—which permits it to be undecidable, unresolvably ambiguous at an abstract level of epistemological analysis, and yet at a concrete level, historically sedimented, set in place, stabilized, appropriated by a particular class, even though such settings, stabilizations, and appropriations will be upset in turn by other classes, other times. In his small history of "rights," Burke shows that the term, as it is embedded in our Bill of Rights, and its prehistory in the Magna Carta and the "reactionary" struggles of the feudal barons against "progressive" centralized authority, is always the focus of historical struggle; that the way the term "rights" is decided is a sure marker of social change and social, economic, and political power, and where that power lies. Burke shrewdly calls the feudal barons' position "reactionary," and he puts "reactionary" within quotation marks not because he sides with the barons but because "reaction" and "progress" in this struggle are always appropriated and deployed by the politically victorious. Later in Burke's history, the role of the feudal reactionaries is played by the progressives of American democracy, but with a difference. Since the dialectically necessary counter-concept of British sovereignty (the Crown itself) has been abolished in our founding documents, we must find a suitable replacement—and we do. Our "rights" are defined against the government elected by the people. Our rights, unlike those defined in the British Bill of Rights, are those of a minority, or of individuals, against the will of a majority or a collectivity. And as Burke shows, this rights/sovereignty dialectic in American history was by no means politically fixed, decided, in the way that the founding fathers decided it in the later eighteenth century. As if looking ahead critically to the current partisans of undecidability, Burke wrote in *The Philosophy of Literary Form*: "the statement that a term [like "rights"] is 'dialectical,' in that it derives its meaning from an opposite term, and that the opposite term may be different at different historical periods does not imply that such terms are 'meaningless.'" Far from it: such terms shape the course of political history because they are used, put into practice with very definite ("decidable") human costs. The epistemological undecidability of discourse is always politically irrelevant, since discourse by definition is always in use, always in force, always ideologically directed. On the other hand, the undecidability of discourse is always, at least in certain hands, very much to the political point, as Burke in so many words tried to indicate, in his meditation on "the people" and the American political idiom, in his address to the American Writers' Congress, because its undecidability makes it always open to interested appropriation: undecidability, then, to anthropomorphize for a moment, as linguistic desire for ideological appropriation.[54]

One final, complicated example that compresses Burke's interests in philosophy, science, and sociopolitical history: I allude to his section on Darwin in the *Grammar* and to an earlier discussion of Darwin in *Attitudes Toward History*. Burke is struck by the preservation, as a kind of historical unconscious, in a period so profoundly committed to liberalism, of a feudalistic mode of thought in the nineteenth century's "extreme emphasis upon *genesis, origin.*"[55] The emphasis on genesis and origin is produced, as he shows in his analysis of Thomism and medieval economics, by a familial metaphor: "From this metaphor there flowed the need of obedience to authority, as embodied in customs. In families one does not 'vote.' Authority does not rise by deputation, as in parliamentary procedure—it is just where it is, being grounded in the magic of custom."[56] By developing this familial perspective to universal limits, Thomism interwove the hegemonic, symbolic architecture of medieval feudalism, a structure uncannily built upon "the foundations of human guilt."[57] The church bureaucracy was pictured as a large-scale replica of family relationships, "with 'fathers,' 'mothers,' 'brothers,' 'sisters,' 'Father,' and 'Mother' (a particularly serviceable pattern in that it readily shunts the erring son into the role of symbolic parricide)."[58] Darwin's formula of the "descent of man" is genealogical (feudalistic) to the core in that it analyzes man "by reference to his parentage: *what he was.*"[59] At one level, at least, what is preserved in Darwin's books, great books of objective knowledge for the liberal nineteenth century, is the political vision of feudalism: the thorough crushing of individual liberty.

If Burke's earlier analysis stresses how a discourse presumably beyond ideology, committed to scientific truth, is strongly marked in its theoretical underpinnings by a Thomist ideology, then his later analysis of Darwin demonstrates that those same texts are marked as well by forms of bourgeois political idealism more contemporary to Darwin's life. The long duration of feudalist hegemony that in one way captured Darwin's writing is resisted and interrupted by a newer hegemony of liberalism. Despite its nominal, programmatic commitment to scenic principles, Darwin's philosophy of deterministic materialism, in which existence can be explained only by its conditions, is invaded by idealistic notions of "purpose" and "agent" that stress a quality of "action" internally motivated and irreducible to the "motions" of environment. Many of Darwin's key terms "lend themselves readily to appeal by ambiguities of the pathetic fallacy."[60] Hence, although his conscious intention (his "act") seems purely materialistic, examination of his discourse reveals that a larger discursive force of intention (what Jameson would call a "political unconscious") that no single subject can control is at work in Darwin's books, binding them over to a liberal political discourse more encompassing even than his own scientific writing—and more encompassing than its purely scientific history of evolutionary thought—even as those books had been bound over in another way to the political discourse of feudalism.

Burke's analysis of this liberal phase of the politics of Darwin's science comes into sharp focus on the occurrence of the term "variability" in *The Origin of Species*. In an effort to deny an internal force of change in an organism, a force appropriate to an autonomous agent, not a thing in context, Darwin finds himself conceding a minimal "tendency to ordinary variability" that cannot be reduced to observable scenic factors.[61] While this pressure of an agent term on his vocabulary points once again to the heraldic or familial perspective of his theory and the consequence that Burke has read out of that metaphor, it also points, as Burke concludes, to the politics of "nineteenth-century English liberalism, in stressing the selective factor of *competition* . . . and in deriving new species from *individual* variations."[62] All this conflict is condensed in an exquisite ambiguity in Darwin's term "variability," which allows simultaneously "for two quite different meanings, . . . one referring to a cause *ab extra* and the other to some internal principle of action. It stands pliantly where scene overlaps upon agent."[63] With his rare integration of the resources of a technical, formalist—even deconstructionist—criticism and those of social and political investigation, in this analysis of the ideological forces of class struggle vying for domination of Darwin's biological texts Burke enacted as a reader of texts a political role for intellectuals that contemporary critical theory can ignore only if it wishes to risk the relevance of its enterprise, only if it continues to insist on its isolation of *logos* from act.

Part Three

$\mathbf{M}$ore than any other book he would write (piece together) *Counter-Statement* embodies Kenneth Burke's political ideals for writing: I mean both "critical" and "literary" writing (a conventionally posited difference he won't respect). *Counter-Statement* was published in 1931. The time of Burke's first theoretical book is really, then, the time of high modernism, but the book's polemical force, as its title indicates, is oppositional at more than one level. In one important sense Burke's "counter-statement" works against the grain of the modernist aesthetic opposition: theories of aesthetic autonomy are an object of his critique here in this early book, as they are everywhere through the books of his middle and later career. His attacks on the ideal of aesthetic privilege and its matrix in social alienation and fragmentation were never, however, propelled out of unsympathetic rear-guard impulses. After all, Burke himself was a charter member of the modernist avant-garde: writer of experimental fiction, first American translator of Thomas Mann, frequent contributor to the little magazines, unswerving champion of Joyce, Williams, and Djuna Barnes—by his late teens, in the company of his high school friend Malcolm Cowley, he had swallowed whole the French Symbolists, Strindberg, Wilde, and even Mencken. Looking back to his high school dreams, he recently said, "It was just like *La Bohème*. We lived for the idea of getting into Greenwich Village."[1]

There is an easy explanation for his criticism of modernism, but it will not do. I refer to the depressingly familiar pattern of the young radical who inevitably turns right as he approaches the mid-life crisis of his late thirties and early forties. The reverse wisdom of Robert Frost speaks more to my point: Burke refused the self-congratulating poses of literary and social radicalism in the 1920s and 1930s (his twenties and thirties as well) in order to protect and nourish a substantial radicalism through his fifties, sixties, seventies, and now well into his eighties. Genuine avant-garde critic that he was and is, Burke has a double intention in his social and literary writings: to work toward the undermining of the sociopolitical order in dominance and, in the same gesture, to assist in the birth of an emergent society. But this Burke, this critical theorist of society, has consistently slipped through our attention. Modernist poets and novelists were grateful for his support, but with their nostalgia for precapitalist forms of society they could not have read him carefully as a social critic. Modernist literary theorists since Cleanth Brooks, and other crusaders for literary autonomy, have been openly hostile—they know better, they sense his more-than-literary commitments. The newest academic avant-garde, from Jacques Derrida to Paul de Man, mainly ignores him: like a powerfully accomplished father, the mere thought of whom creates those queasy feelings of impotence, Burke must be forgotten. He knew too much, too soon.

What Burke knew—what made him both a subtle and sympathetic critic of modernism, a troublesome eccentric to the New Critics and the traditional academic establishment, a traitor to a certain type of thirties' Marxist, and an anxiety and embarrassment to most deconstructionists—was political. But to say that he "knew" the political is already to say too much and to mystify his work as an oppositional thinker. It is to imply that Burke had mastered (as no one else had) a sacred body of knowledge whose proper application would illumine the dark and socially irresponsible realms of modernist literature and criticism: that Burke, in other words, was honestly engaged while others were following the escapist routes marked out in the 1890s or were toying, as

Yeats, Eliot, and Pound had toyed, with the fascist adventure. Politically oriented literary criticism, especially in its radical vein, has a hard time getting beyond the category of "false consciousness," but what Burke knew and what from early on he was able to show, with stunning insight and generosity, was that the political is not something we need to achieve—like some ultimate, advanced degree certifying that we have passed through false consciousness to the highest humanity of vision. Burke had invested too heavily in the modernist enterprise to indulge that curious blend of dogmatism and sentimentality sometimes packaged with the label of Marxism; he had read his Marx too closely to make that kind of mistake.

Unlike most of his literary contemporaries (and ours) and their progenitors, Burke, though tempted, never bought the separatism that isolated action from contemplation, willing from imagining, or poetry from power. He was never captured by the political self-disenfranchisement of literary intellectuals rationalized by a certain reading of Kant's tripartist system (later celebrated in de Man's culminating essays on rhetoric). For what Burke knew was not a particular political imperative; he had something more powerful, something I take to be fundamental to any sophisticated political consciousness: the understanding that all intellectual activity (even the most theoretical sort that disdains politics) is itself, from the start, a kind of praxis. Very simply: intellectual activity is first and foremost for Burke an *act*. Without for a moment forsaking the deconstructive complexities of "act" and "substance" that he had uncovered in his *Grammar*, Burke will insist that the intellectual act is involved in power in every way— caught up in it, used by interests not at all intellectual, itself generating power—and, however innocently, promoting, shoring up, binding itself over to power, even, on occasion, criticizing or resisting ruling forces and their institutional loci in the society that most modern literary intellectuals need to think they view from afar, from on high, and in perfect contempt. However internally fissured and contradictory, however ensnared in and identified with contexts (political and philosophical) beyond its awareness, however ignorant of, and out of its control, the consequences of its activities (I cite the major banalities of contemporary theory's repression of the political), no degree of shrewd application of strategies of reading that stress aporia, *mise en*

abyme, undecidability, and other techniques of textual interpretation can possibly call back, neutralize, or in any way forestall the
effects of force unleashed by the act of the mind. The reason for
this is in essence quite simple: we have readers, and they receive
our impact. In that book which is profoundly embarrassing for all
main-line ideologies of modernist and post-modernist theory—I
refer to *A Rhetoric of Motives*—Burke puts it this way, striking
through cleanly to the timid heart of the matter: "Any specialized
activity participates in a larger unit of action. 'Identification' is a
word for the autonomous activity's place in this wider context, a
place with which the agent may be unconcerned. The shepherd
[how wicked of him to choose this metaphor] *qua* shepherd, acts
for the good of the sheep, to protect them from discomfiture and
harm. But he may be 'identified' with a project that is raising the
sheep for market."[2]

Burke's work may be read as an attempt to explode the myth of
disinterest. His definition as a political thinker may be located
precisely in his effort to place our "autonomous" activities as
intellectuals within the larger capitalist project whose purpose is
always to prepare the sheep for market. His range and acuteness
as a thinker in Marx's tradition may be measured initially by
another passage from his *Rhetoric*: "the extreme division of labor
under late capitalist liberalism having made dispersion the norm
and having transformed the state of Babel into an ideal, the true
liberal must view almost as an affront the Rhetorical concern with
identification whereby the principles of a specialty cannot be
taken at their face value, simply as the motives proper to that
speciality. They *are* motives proper to the specialty *as such*, but
not to the specialty as *participant in a wider context of motives*."[3]

In *Counter-Statement* Burke takes his stand within modernism
(witness his celebration of Flaubert, Pater, De Gourmont, Mann,
and Gide) but only in order to drive modernism toward political
and social consequences that he regards as inherent in its project
though not often intended and certainly not often wanted. By
choosing a word loaded with powerful significance in religious
and political history in order to describe what art does—the word
is "antinomian"—Burke shrewdly establishes his difference with
the aestheticist doctrine at the heart of modernist theory: art
is not a kind of distinctive substance, or a world apart, a unique
sort of linguistic being, but, rather, a type of oppositional activity

in the world, a discordant and disruptive voice out to "undermine any one rigid scheme of living."[4] From the beginning, aestheticist theory is for Burke as much social theory as it is art theory, and his main intention in *Counter-Statement* is to consider what "social structure would have to become" if the antinomian aesthetic were to prevail. "What," he asks as an aesthetic pragmatist, "could be the particular results of this particular 'aesthetic'?"[5] With little fanfare in the preface to the first edition of *Counter-Statement*, Burke deftly makes the point that literary and art theory since Kant generally eludes: you can theorize all you want about an autonomous form of discourse that cannot be touched by the practical world, but your theorizing is itself a form of action. Whether there is such a thing as autonomous art is the object of speculation; the speculative act is not, however, itself autonomous. So the question that Burke asks us is not what social structure might become if autonomous art were to prevail (he does not believe in any such thing) but what social structure is implied by a certain type of modernist theorizing about art.

1

Burke's earliest and most persistent definition of form ("the creation of an appetite in the mind of an auditor, and the adequate satisfying of that appetite") is rhetorical in the classical tradition; it forms the basis of his theory of reading.[6] Form is neither free, as formalists would have it, an objective configuration independent of its producers and receivers, inhering somehow in linguistic substance alone; nor is it a subjective imposition, as psychologistic thinkers would see it, inhering wholly in the mind of an auditor. Form is a relationship of manipulation between a text and an audience—a relationship (here is Burke's post-Nietzschean contribution to classical rhetorical tradition) in which power is, in the same moment, given both its birth and its point of application. On behalf of Burke we must say that there is no literary power outside the text, but we may say so only on condition that we understand that there is no text outside the rhetorical relation; that the definition of text, and textuality, must include the factor of its reception; and that reception is always firmly planted in the historical world. Form inheres in the rhetorical relation because form creates that relationship: formalism is merely the abstraction of technique from the context of power that lends it its significance. Form, rhetoric, and power—and by easy implication domination, resistance, and ideology—these are the major Burkean themes opened in *Counter-Statement*. In the essay "Psychology and Form" he broaches the theory of rhetorical form mainly in readings of passages from *Hamlet* and *The Waste Land*; he fills the theory out in "The Poetic Process" and then elaborates it in exhaustive detail in the great set piece, what he called his "machine for criticism," the "Lexicon Rhetoricae."

Now, if we limit our inquiry to these three pieces—and they are the obvious places to look for Burke's theory of rhetoric in *Counter-Statement*—the portrait of Burke that we are likely to come away with is one of a thinker who would resist the apolitical excesses of modernism but was in fact appropriated by a late and candid version of the traditional (and historically most powerful) idea of the "literary," initially established in Aristotle's *Poetics* and reiterated in many guises since then. Almost always overtly opposed to the historical and the rhetorical (and therefore to the political), the idea of the literary as the uncontingent, the universal, a kind of mimesis that is always pretty much above it all, has dominated, and continues to dominate, the history of criticism. (Often unconsciously, but sometimes with covert intention, the traditional idea of mimesis, as representation of the universal, is in the service of a traditional political vision grounded on a vertically structured society—but that is another story, which I cannot develop here.) The extreme but representative feelings of that giant of modernism, W. B. Yeats (rhetoric is "the will trying to do the work of the imagination"), are apparently accommodated by Burke's theory of rhetorical form: in spite of his keen eye for manipulation and power, in spite of his desire to locate the literary in a transaction between writer and audience (he defines literature as written or spoken words "designed for the express purpose of arousing emotions"), Burke's idea of rhetoric and power, in its best known formulations, would satisfy that inhuman Platonic censor internalized by literary theory ever since Aristotle (in a gesture of appeasement to his master from which literary study has not yet recovered) tried to segregate poetry and history.[7]

Let me try to contextualize Burke's problem by radically reducing the history of literary theory to the names "Aristotle" and "Kant," which I want to function not as signs of individual authors but as forces of literary desire. "Aristotle," then, is the name of a desire (its *locus classicus* is the ninth chapter of the *Poetics*) to free literary representations from the sort of particularity that would tie them to the specifications of history: a literary representation properly plotted earns the right to be called "universal" because it is governed by laws of human probability and necessity that are as compelling (in the thinking of "Aristotle") as the laws of nature. Although the name of "Kant" is linked in the history of philosophy with a "Copernican" revolution that reversed the epistemological principles of the real Aristotle, in the realm of literary and general aesthetic theory, as it is conventionally understood, it functions as a reinforcement of the desire of "Aristotle." By attempting to take the aesthetic rigorously away from willing, cognition, and all *interest*, "Kant" assures "Aristotle" that literary representation can never be politicized by the temporal powers that operate in society. Let me extend, and conclude, this little story by saying that there is a third desire (stubborn, rhetorical, poor relation of "Aristotle," consistent, guilty afterthought of most theories of mimesis) that we can label with the name "Horace." It is the forbidden desire for power (no humanist likes to admit to it), for domination and for relevance in the blurred, hegemonic sphere of the cultural-political. In the rhetorical tradition—and what could be more appropriate?—the desire that I have called "Horace" is repressed, and abrasive terms like "power" and "domination" are sugared over with cunning words like "utility," "guidance," and "teaching"—especially teaching.

Burke's problem is this: the literary as the rhetorical is reprised and foregrounded in *Counter-Statement*, and given some real political backbone, but then is quickly made over into a transcendental, as if Burke's goal were to make rhetoric safe for modernism. If we can identify the main line of literary defense since the Greeks with a desire to hide history and power, then perhaps we can take the measure of that desire's astonishing stamina by noting that Burke is sucked into the conventional idea of the literary in the very act of working against it. If his revisionary idea of literary form as the linchpin of textual power (it makes possible a different reading of Longinus) jars against traditional literary thought, we have to admit that at one level anyway Burke's intention would appear to prohibit textual power from political involvement. Contradictory as such a suggestion will sound, I think it necessary to characterize one level of his theory as a *rhetoric of nature*, with his emphasis on rhetoric moving us deeply into the affairs of the world that we make, even as his emphasis on unchanging, culturally and historically unmodifiable capacities of response would seem to move us beyond.

It is in Burke's understanding of "audience" that we can pinpoint the difficulty. This key material condition for rhetorical discourse, this human object of a discourse of power-with-a-design, is oddly Platonized, via a Kantian anthropology, so that all rhetorical moves are geared toward a natural ground for form. Like many a good modernist before him (Mallarmé is the model), Burke treasures the referential deserts of music. The rhetoric of music, Burke's paradigm for aesthetic form in general, is rooted not in "information" (which music is not much fit to impart) but in an "eloquence" generated by the writer's ability to tap patterns of emotion that Burke characterizes variously as "natural," as "racial appetites," as "innate forms of the mind"—all inherent "in the very germ plasm of man."[8] Therefore the entire gamut of actual aesthetic effects (crescendo, contrast, comparison, balance, repetition, disclosure, reversal, contraction, expansion, magnification, etc.) are realizations in sensuous media of ideal subjective categories that constitute the conditions of literary appeal. "For we need but take . . . [Plato's] universals out of heaven and situate them in the human mind (a process begun by Kant), making them not metaphysical but psychological. . . . these potentialities are continually changing their external aspects, their 'individuations,' [but] they do not change in essence."[9] Of course they don't: "essences" are precisely those sorts of things which can't change and still be essences.

Through Burke, Mallarmé's symbolist project (who would have believed it?) captures the dangerous historical antagonist of literary mimesis, rhetoric itself, and the victory of the literary over history and politics would appear absolute. The true rhetorician, like Count Axel, leaves the politics to his servants: the

destiny of the higher rhetoric is the destiny that modernist poetics from Kant through Mallarmé and the New Critics always
imagined for itself. The world is left to the dirty politicians (a
redundancy), to the journalists, to the writers of naturalist and
realist fiction, and most of all (this theme *ad nauseam*), it is left to
the scientists, who for most modernists (early Burke is no exception) are the rulers of information—what the Yeats of the 1890s,
in the manner of Villiers de L'Isle-Adam, tellingly called mere
"externality."[10] For modernists, the goal is an essentialized
world, now in the theory of Burke understood not as some other
world (the spiritualism of the young Yeats is really symptomatic
of modernism's basic urge for aesthetic transcendence) or as
some frozen aesthetic discourse (Joseph Frank called it spatial
form). The world of essence in Burke's modernism is defined by
the concerns of a certain kind of reception theory: by the abiding
patterns of human subjectivity whose universal structures bind
us all across the ages, cultures, and societies, even as writers who
utilize those patterns are bound to each other in a "tradition"
(such binding being the basis of tradition understood as a product of rhetoric), forming a community whose persistence and
value are guaranteed by the subjective human foundations of
their work. For all its desire to articulate the pure, fresh break
with tradition, to be original, free, and autonomous, modernism
joins the main line of humanist literary theory. By bringing a
potentially dangerous rhetorical theory into the fold of modernist
thought, by enclosing rhetoric, which historically never had any
fear of the so-called *outside* of literature (Yeats's "externality") in
the symbolist sanctuary of subjectivity itself, Burke becomes
modernism's cagiest champion. That, I believe, is the strongest
political case that can be made against the work of Kenneth
Burke. With friends like Burke, rhetoric needs no enemies. Not
content to leave the rhetorical and the political to men of will,
modernism in Burke would overreach to aestheticize rhetoric
itself. In that proleptic moment in *Counter-Statement*, the false
break called the postmodern (which we might mark in critical
theory by de Man's deliberately depoliticizing essays on rhetoric)
folds back into modernism, even as modernism folds back into a
traditional defense of the literary.

   Burke's Kantian-anthropological stress on patterns of subjectivity, a shared inner world, a democracy of subjectivities that

defies all specified social and historical location, is finally not, however, apolitical—it is utopian, but a utopia with no possibility of objective realization in a world of affairs that is regarded as stubborn, alienating facticity. Here is still another paralyzing version of the dissociation of sensibility, of the subject-object split that has haunted modern thought since Descartes. Some time in the early seventeenth century, the space of the essentially human begins to be constricted in literary and philosophical circles to the sphere of alienated subjectivity—withdrawn from practice and limited to an appropriately interiorized aesthetic dimension. Yeats is again useful at this point: rhetoric, he says, is the quarrel we have with others; poetry the quarrel we have with ourselves. Burke's apolitical modernist move is, then, archetypally political in the way that the aesthetic has been political since Addison's essays on the pleasures of imagination or Young's discourse on the values of original composition: the aesthetic as refusal of the life actually conducted in actual society.

2

Of course the flight from actual politics in early Burke might well represent the best modernist literary case for him, and surely that is not startling news since, with the exception of its rhetorical vein, too much of the history of criticism might be said to represent inadvertently the best political case against literary study. If we can be critical of Burke for being too much of an insider, then, at the same time, we have to say that his strength as a political thinker for literary critics also in part resides there. If all intellectual activity is a kind of praxis, a primary Burkean axiom, then no less so is the activity of literary theory when it seems most irrelevant to political and social interests. Burke understood this better perhaps than any other literary thinker in the twentieth century. Hence these essays in *Counter-Statement*: "The Status of Art," his "Program," and the "Lexicon Rhetoricae," which, though they explore and press themes in apparent contradiction to those we have seen in "Psychology and Form" and "The Poetic

Process," in effect present us with an issue more interesting and more profound than the issue of intellectual contradiction. Taken as a whole, *Counter-Statement* represents a modernist variation on the dominant theme in the history of criticism since the late eighteenth century (aesthetic isolationism) and the most urgent integrationist response to that depressing stance of the literary intellectual. And most compellingly for his literary readers, Burke demonstrates in *Counter-Statement*, by dramatic example, that the most convincing way out of aesthetic isolationism is the way through.

The issue of the relation of aesthetics to politics, which is the true subject of "The Status of Art," might best be focused for us by the lens of *Das Kapital*: "nothing," Marx wrote there, "can be a value without being an object of utility. If the thing is useless, so is the labor contained in it; the labor does not count as labor, and therefore creates no value."[11] Because his critique of modern society is sometimes delivered ironically, in the voice of capitalism, Marx's own cultural ideals are often confused (especially by academic defenders of literature) with the achieved aims of capitalism. It may not therefore be altogether out of place to say here that in the passage just quoted Marx was not endorsing the economic reductionism of capitalism, nor would he endorse the economism often promoted in his name. At one level in this passage Marx is describing the genesis of (exchange) value from utility value. He is saying that if we assume the utility value of a given object, we can trace the movement to value via the necessary commodification of labor. To steal a phrase from Wallace Stevens, that is old song. At a less apparent level, which we reach by bringing the corpus of Marx to bear on this passage (I am insisting, against Louis Althusser, that we read with no break inserted between *Capital* and the work prior to 1845), Marx projects a critical image of a grimly narrowed, reified life in which *use* (understood only in its most fundamental of life-supporting senses) dominates the definitions of value and human productivity. Though this is not the place to argue it, a decent reading of *Capital* should urge that, with the most passionate defenders of aesthetic privilege and the life of the spirit, Marx (though no defender of aesthetic privilege) understood that there was more to life, labor, and value than *that*. The passage from *Capital* (especially with hindsight) sets the stage for a broad-based criticism of the degraded life of the spirit promoted by capitalism's economic principles, and positions us to judge modernist literature and literary theory not as they are often judged, either in narrowly "committed" quarters or in the typical modernist theoretical self-characterizations pronounced in any number of manifestos and apologies. If we can put these categories of judgment aside, we may read modernism as a critically engaged rhetoric, a response to the conditions of our lives that capitalist imperatives have established, ingrained, and, with terrific stamina, massively sustained.

With impressive accuracy in the essay "The Status of Art," Burke traces the careening, apparently uncontrolled polemical moves of modernist aesthetic thought as it switches its critical intentions from (1) something like the socioeconomic point of Marx's critique of capitalism to (2) a grandiose (yet critical) art for life's sake claim for aesthetic independence, a claim for the aesthetic as a preserve of unique human value that, if only we can contact it and properly treasure it, will surely redeem our existence by freeing us from the deadly hold of all nonaesthetic authorities; and then, from such grandeur of aesthetic claim to (3) another, more familiar, self-trivializing, even self-invalidating claim of autonomy without point: art for art's sake. Burke's evaluation of these various polemical emphases proceeds from his understanding of the hostile social context that unifies the intentions of modernism. Art is said to be "purposiveness without purpose"; it is said to be "play"; it is said to be "refuge"; it is said to be "amoral"; it is said to be "pure"; it is said to be "symbolic." In the nineteenth and twentieth centuries, art is said to be all these things because it is thought that art cannot be "purposive," or "useful," or "work," or "involved," or "moral," or, as opposed to symbolic, "logical." To put it as sympathetically as I can: from the point of view of the aesthetic defense, what is generally regarded as "moral" or as "work" since the advent of industrial capitalism—the moral life, the useful life—has for excellent reasons become wholly repulsive to the humanist intellectual. The defensiveness of modernism's defenders, as Burke notes, takes on the appearance of a "last stand."[12]

More troubling yet, art's defenders permit art's (capitalist) detractors to set the terms of debate by establishing the ruling antithesis of value (work vs. play) as a not-so-hidden hierarchy. In the nineteenth and twentieth centuries, theories of art and literature attempt, at a level only perhaps half-conscious, to function rhetorically in an effort directed in some part toward the negation of the powerfully operating imperatives of use and labor dominating industrial societies. Consequently, putative aesthetic virtues like "play" and "purity" must all be read through the covert ethicopractical categories of amorality and uselessness: as potential replacements of the repugnant shopkeeper values that were being enthroned under capitalism, as domains of value, maybe even vague yearnings for a new society, a new understanding of morality and use somehow situated outside all bourgeois intellectual horizons. Kant's aesthetic, with its emphasis on "purposiveness without purpose," a category that signifies the debunking of willing, utility, and rhetoric, marks the first major appearance of a philosophical consciousness whose intention (if not achievement) is heavily critical. For unlike the Kant known to the usual histories of aesthetic theory, the Kant that I am putting forward now with Burke's help stood for aesthetic autonomy not for itself (as is the case with his academic formalist progeny—their name is legion) but because such autonomy was a refusal of what he saw the will accomplishing in the social formation within which his writing and thinking took place. This Kant is not only a bourgeois theorist (as Lukács claimed) but also an embryonic critical theorist of society.[13]

The heady socialist vision of freedom that Marx had evoked toward the end of the third volume of *Capital*—a realm "where labor which is in fact determined by necessity and mundane considerations ceases," a realm that cannot be situated on the terrain of any of the social formations and modes of production known in history, a realm in which human energy, no longer ruled by nature, becomes "an end in itself"—this "in itself," this mark of freedom, may represent no more, or less, than the full socialization and historical realization of the aesthetic vision of freedom that Kant had evoked at the heart of his third *Critique*: an experience similarly independent of nature, of all interest, of all end-seeking, all laboring activity—all determination—a good in itself unimaginable in a consciousness of value dominated (as Kant's was not) by the commodity and by the structure of value determined by the commodity.[14] I am arguing, on the side of Herbert Marcuse, that Marx's realm of freedom and Kant's aesthetic are fraternal alternatives to what work had become in the nineteenth century. Neither "play" nor "work," in other words, are innocent terms in the Kantian system, for play represents (Schiller would pick this up) visionary social hope for an aesthetic "state" ruptured from the actual state of society in which working has become, for most, degradation and alienation. However crippled by his inability to see the aesthetic state as an effect or production of the unfolding cooperation of labor, as a historical possibility of social change or, more guardedly, as an indispensable instrument for a thoroughgoing socialist critique of capitalism (rather than as utopian alternative to society and history), Kant's aesthetic yet represented an effort of philosophical intervention. Burke's summary of the weakness of such an intervention—and Kant can be made to stand for all aesthetic critics of capitalist society, including Marcuse—makes the ironic point: "in an age when 'work' was becoming one of society's basic catchwords, art could not very well be associated with play without some loss of prestige."[15] The main line of aesthetic theory since Kant develops from its accurate reading of the alienating message of capitalist hegemony. Kantian, symbolist, and aestheticist patterns of thought, all of which father modernist political refusals, originate in gestures of worldly negation that are political through and through.

The questions that Burke as insider poses repeatedly are strategically practical: Can an aesthetic politics of negation have any substantial effect? Can such a politics make anyone (aside from aesthetes) care for the values of art? Can it make anything happen? Can social change be a result of the naughty, theatrical gestures of Bohemians? Has the modernist defense of the aesthetic done anything more than to cause artists, writers, literary theorists, and university teachers of literature to be even more embattled? Can the repeated assertions of Flaubert of his mighty toil, can the numbing repetitions (like some sort of incantation) of the phrase "work of art" be received by an assembly line worker with anything but a guffaw? If literary writing is a kind of work (hard work at that: no one who writes will deny it), but work that does not in the main produce commodities, then what is the *result* of writing, and what place can aesthetic production take, if not a place of irrelevance, in a society that worships the commodity?

Burke approaches these questions by distinguishing rejection theories of aestheticist cast from reflection theories of determinist origin. If modernist aesthetic would engender, as nascent utopian political activity, a radical rupture with its social context, then its negative in aesthetic theory that develops alongside it in the nineteenth century, positivist and naturalist accounts, would shore up and help to sustain the status quo. (The social rage and reformism of naturalist and realist novelists is a fact, but their fictions tend to project an image of the real as hopeless inevitability, beyond ministration.) Burke's attack on rejection theories is many-sided. Art for art's sake theorists he would confront with the humiliating social context of World War I: "Disciples of Art for Art's Sake might advocate art as a refuge, a solace for the grimness about them, but the spirit of social mockery could no longer fit the scene. One can mock death, but one cannot mock men in danger of death. In the presence of so much disaster, there was no incentive to call art disastrous."[16] To those who, with Flaubert's attorney, would argue for the immunity of art from charges of immorality by claiming art's innocence as "unmoral," Burke says that in a society in which utility is king "unmorality was in the end a much greater danger to the prestige of art than immorality could ever have been, since it implied once again the ineffectiveness of art."[17] And against those who would define the opposing forces socially as a bourgeois-Bohemian conflict, he brings a variety of powerful responses. Baudelaire may outrage the bourgeoisie not because he is an avant-garde presager of a new society but because he brings against bourgeois standards the values of a residual culture, of an older society that the bourgeoisie wanted to discredit. "Baudelaire courts poverty, lamentation, sullenness, a discipline of internal strife; his concerns are the concerns of an early Christian anchorite voluntarily placing himself in jeopardy—and what could be more 'conservative' than this, what more unlike the young Californian with his benign circle of culture, progress, and prosperity, or his football conception of discipline?"[18] Bohemian opposition, at any rate, tended to be "more picturesque than ominous." Wilde, Burke argues, "is as responsible as anyone for the weakening of the bourgeois-Bohemian conflict. The next generation of authors married at twenty, courted the strictest conventionality of dress and manners, and tended to consider a few years in business as the new educational equivalent of the European tour."[19]

From a political standpoint, the most paralyzing feature of the bourgeois-Bohemian conflict was the alliance of Bohemians with the symbolist aesthetic. For Burke the alogical symbolist method of connecting ideas, images, and feelings represented a real and important departure in the history of poetic method. But it is just there, in his innovativeness as an artist, that the symbolist writer failed as an intellectual: "he was not matching his imaginative experiments with their equivalents in critical theory. . . . Far from pleading with his public, the artist heightened his antagonism: hence his readiness to *épater le bourgeois*. Art now took on a distinctly obscurantist trait, not because it was anymore 'obscure' than previous art (nothing is more obscure than an afterdinner speaker's distinctions between optimism and over optimism, yet no one is troubled by them) but because the public had not been schooled as to just wherein the clarity of such art was to be sought."[20] Burke's point that symbolist writers failed as critical theorists needs a little translation: symbolist imaginative writing failed to make its impact, he is arguing, because symbolist writers were irresponsible to themselves—they refused their necessary roles as intellectuals, as educators ("the public had not been schooled") who might have been able to construct bridges between the (always) small pockets of the avant-garde and the greater public. The symbolists failed to teach their potential (wider) public how to *read*; therefore they failed to teach it how to *think*; and therefore they failed to shape its modes of *action*. However, the failure to act intellectually within the broader social context (no one would deny that symbolists taught each other how to read) is itself an act. The avant-garde writer could speak forcefully, as Marx had, of the alienating economic structure of his society. But his failure to intervene critically (in two senses of the word) amounts to an *act*—one of self-trivialization.

When Burke turns his attention from rejection to reflection theories, he remarks that he is entering upon a terrain even more hostile to art's potential as social criticism. What he calls "causation" theories—naturalist and psychoanalytic accounts, those of positivists, historical relativists, of Taine, Spengler, and what we would call "vulgar Marxists"—all such accounts, in a variety of ways and in a fashion directly in opposition to the style of avant-gardists, have the effect of neutralizing the artist as an intellectual. The avant-gardist falls into political quietism and irrelevance because of his failure to actualize his potential as an intellectual disseminator of critical values. And perhaps on this issue of critical failure we can do no better than to appeal to Georg

Lukács's explanation of the ideology of modernism. If the modernist conceives of his alienation not as a specific social fate but as the human condition, then what could possibly be the point of intervention? By choosing to work within determinist schemes of art, the reflectionist will also have to accept quietism as a necessary consequence of his aesthetic choice. The reflectionist must accept from the outset the impossibility of a critical intelligence—a consciousness not already utterly constituted by its environment. Burke reserves his most searching and suggestive refutation of causation doctrine for the type that in the parodic form of Marxism called "economist" grossly simplified the concept of social context to "exclude all but political and economic factors"—especially economic factors. Vulgar Marxism says: "Changes in art occur concomitantly with changes in political and economic conditions; therefore the changes in art are caused by the changes in political and economic conditions."[21]

Burke had tough times with American Marxists in the 1930s because his understanding of Marx wouldn't permit him to make those kinds of reductions. The one-way determinism of the base/superstructure model of society enthrones the economic and violates his sense of organic wholeness, of interdependence, and most of all it violates his sense of the real power of cultural expression. His response to the reduction of Marx is devastating:

> Now, it is not very sound dialectic to assume that, because two things change concomitantly, one can be called exclusively a cause of the other. If mere concurrence can prove causation, why could not an opponent assume from the same facts that the changes in art and ideas caused the changes in economic conditions? We know, for example, that the feminist "aesthetic" served as preparation for the enfranchisement of women: here is an obvious example of an attitude's affecting a change in social structure.[22]

With the charge that economist Marxism is undialectical, Burke one-ups his critics on the official left of the 1930s and, in the same moment, raises the aesthetic to the decisive sphere of hegemonic function where the war over the political formation of consciousness is fought out. In one move, both rejectionists and reflectionists are shunted aside. With the representations of popular culture, with the press and other so-called media of information, with educational and religious institutions, with the family and with political parties, artistic production takes its place in the political process. Political engagement is not something after the fact, as if art's "pleasure" needed to be rationalized by some up-dated Horatian formula, its joyful being made somehow proper: as if art could not be trusted on its own terms to be anything but an erotic explosion in the dark. In the language of poststructuralist theory, but against its intention, Burke is saying that there is "always already" more at stake than the pleasure of the text. Art is "always already" action within the highly active hegemonic process that produces our consent to dominant power (our values, our world views, our choices and all power-serving ideological "truths" that we accept unreflectively). Art is an instrument, one of the powers that create us as sociopolitical beings.

To say that artistic activity has that kind of force within society is not equivalent to saying that it has oppositional force. Art may operate as a force for change, even conceivably as a force for revolution; on the other hand, it may operate to sustain the status quo of ruling power, or, worse yet, it may operate as an agent of reaction. Burke's example of feminist aesthetic is an example of the liberating sort. Here is another example:

> For what is our advertising, what is our "success" fiction in the average commercial magazine, what are our cinematic representations of the "good life," but a vast method of determining the criteria of a nation, and thus its conduct, by the assistance of art? And if, as in modern warfare, the fundamental aspirations of our "pure" scientists are derided, similarly in the rise of art to promote a belief in the primary cultural value of material acquisition, the fundamental aspirations of the pure artist are derided. The proper complaint, here, however, is not that art has been ineffective, but that a certain brand of art has been only too effective.[23]

To the high modernist aesthete, to the typical thirties Marxist in the United States, and to the academic traditionalist who believes in literature's high human destiny—its freedom from the grubby world of advertising—this passage must have been and must still be an affront. Like pure science, pure art will be *used*, whatever the intentions of pure artist and pure scientist. Art's rhetorical function is inescapable. In the instance that Burke cites, the precious aesthetic techniques of Bohemian opposition are manipulated in order to determine conduct and belief in such a way that consumerism is reinforced and promoted. The conventional Marxist must find Burke enigmatic, for he is arguing that in some part art determines social life (Wilde wasn't all wrong) even though dogma says that it must be the other way around. Against the grain of conventional Marxism, with its reflectionist view of culture grounded on the base/superstructure metaphor, Burke is saying that art has an organic role to play in the economy and that it plays that role by acting as the cultural fuel for the machine of consumer capitalism. And the conventional literary academic can only be outraged by Burke's deliberate vulgarization of "literature" to mean any use of language that has the effect of shaping and controlling attitudes and behavior.

There is a kernel of truth in the formalist's claim for the formal self-sufficiency of the literary text, but ultimately it is not a truth that will please formalists. Form qua form (Burke defines the varieties thereof in his "Lexicon") is unto itself because it is ideologically empty and untouched by power. Purity of form exists only as an abstraction in the mind of the formalist. The formalist truth about form can therefore only confirm Burke's theory of rhetoric, for its significance stipulates that form is always a thing to be appropriated (always on the way to appropriation) by the political process conceived in its broad hegemonic sense. And there is no room at all here for sentimentality; art lends itself equally to ugly as well as to desirable political processes. Burke's essay on Hitler, for example, is offered as an essay on literary artistry. I think that we can see now how Burke's earlier rhetoric of nature becomes a rhetoric of aesthetic power. I am speaking of a power of representation much more pervasive than what is thought to belong exclusively to Milton, Keats, or any of the specialized and canonized writers we call poets or novelists. This power is born in the linkage of form with ideology in its two psychosocial domains: ideology, in other words, both as overt "culture," however "upside down"—a common, normalizing and socializing space, a conscious nodus of beliefs, attitudes, and judgments—and as the sort of unconscious that Althusser called a "lived relation to the world." In neither sense is ideology deterministic and homogeneous, free from the stresses of internal contradiction, which means that in the combined sense of the term, the possibility of struggle and resistance is never in advance eliminated. In the moment of linkage, form would seize and direct ideological substance, transform it into power over the subject-audience; it would turn our ideology, in both senses, over to a disciplinary intention that would utilize and subjugate us. The aesthetic moment of linkage, then, is the manipulative moment at which the subject-audience is submitted ("subjected") to the productive force of ideology.[24] And the act of linking form with ideology is what inserts the writer into the process of sociopolitical education and activates us as his political "subjects." So defined, form is "correct"—Burke, an aesthetic pragmatist, means that it works—when it controls as it gratifies the needs it arouses.[25] Form can both gratify and control those needs, however, only if it properly engages and represents what readers consider desirable and only if the readers' overt ideologies are in some way "respected." Only then can those ideologies be manipulated in the engagement with form so that the power effect touched off by that engagement will engender two ultimate political effects of aesthetic power: the domination effect or its contrary, the effect of resistance.

One very schematic example, with more range to it than Burke might have intended, will have to do:

> As . . . [an] instance of how the correctness of form depends upon the ideology, we may consider a piece of juvenile fiction for Catholic boys. The hero will be consistently a hero: he will show bravery, honesty, kindness to the oppressed, strength in sports, gentleness to women—in every way, by the tenets of repetitive form, he will repeat the fact that he is a hero. And among these repetitions will be his converting of Indians to Catholicism. To a Catholic boy, this will be one more repetition of his identity as an ideal hero; but to the Protestant boy, approaching the work from a slightly different ideology, repetitive form will be endangered at this point.[26]

What is formally "correct" (repetitive) for the Catholic reader will be perhaps formally "incorrect" (discontinuous) for the Protestant reader. Insofar as Catholic readers will be encouraged to understand that the activity of converting others to the faith is continuous with nonsectarian virtues like honesty and gentleness with women, the Catholic reader will be subjected, by the Catholic writer, through literary form, to a power that would rule his behavior by coercing it in a direction that Catholic culture considers desirable. The Catholic reader's ideology is foregrounded and enhanced by a writer who reinforces the habits of thought and action of a particular culture. On the other hand, because his ideology is not precisely enough respected, the Protestant reader must either resist the cultural power expressed by the story, or subtly submit to it by accepting the literary form as repetitive. Unwittingly, in this last instance the Protestant reader would take a crucial literary step down the road to religious conversion.

In order to extend this meditation on culture, writing, and power, let us imagine that Burke had written the following: "And among these repetitions will be the American Catholic's burning of his draft card, his refusal to kill Vietnamese, his desertion to Canada." Furthermore, in order to make such actions attractive, ideologically compelling, let us imagine that the writer linked them, in a repetitive structure, with acts of kindness to the oppressed and the conversion of Indians to the faith. Here, then, would be another kind of example, one that would demonstrate how the adversarial writer might activate within the hegemony in dominance, within the ideology in force, a cultural power (in the name of Catholicism) that would work toward a counter-hegemony—a move against the dominant culture through that very culture's values. If my example is too romantic, then all we need to do is alter it slightly: the Catholic youth cheerfully accepts his tour in Vietnam; the Catholic reader in turn accepts that episode in the story as repetitive of other more obvious Catholic episodes; Catholic interests are thereby made to serve interests not at all religious in nature; political rule is served aesthetically. Either way, within Burke's theory—depending on what you think humane—artistic production is a dangerous or a desirable thing: it makes something happen.

Literature makes something happen—if we need to create a slogan for Burke, then that would probably do better than any other. For one thing, it sums up his doctrine of literary rhetoric; for another, as an allusion to the history of modern critical theory which would negate the formalist credo it calls forth, it situates Burke as an adversarial thinker within the adversarial thinking called "modernist." With a thinker as historically specific and heterogeneous as Burke, it is dangerous to generalize. But his political, ideological, and power-conscious theorizing, especially in the example I have just cited, demands some generalizations, at least of the limiting sort. I have in mind generalizations that have not been welcome in the various houses of formalism. Such as: every text, both in its creation and reception, is ideologically specific as is every subject-reader. Or this one: if the ideology of the text and the ideology of the reader do not overlap in some substantial way, the reading experience, as Burke has been describing it, will not take place, or it will barely take place. Reading in the brute sense, of course, will go on, but power will not be unleashed; the political process in its aesthetic phase will not be activated. The reader will be mainly bored by what he reads because his lived relation to the world will not have been sufficiently engaged. If we can recall here Burke's deconstruction of the "subject" and of "act" in his *Grammar*, we may conclude that the ideological heterogeneity of his decentered subject ensures that textual effects of domination and resistance can never be monolithic, that the ends of writing cannot in advance be known. To say this is to say that a counter-hegemonic effect of political struggle is always a textual possibility.

But the screw of Burkean reception theory must be turned one more time. If Burke's emphasis on rhetoric-as-aesthetic stresses the self-conscious, manipulative work of the writer who knows what he is about, then his adducing of an unconscious—the fuller consequences of which I'll explore later in the text—says not only that the effect of aesthetic force cannot be known in advance but that an unconscious at play in writing and reception will ensure that at some level aesthetic effect is out of control—beyond the purview of traditional rhetoric—and that the "change" in the "social" directed by the aesthetic may not be the change that we writers and receivers want. Rhetoric is the "use of words by human agents to form attitudes or to induce action in other human agents." But what if we don't know quite what we are doing when we use words? What if we don't know who we are? If an ideology, as Burke says, "is an aggregate of beliefs sufficiently at odds with one another to justify opposite kinds of conduct," then under aesthetic pressure it may not be clear how we will act.[27]

What Burke's theory of the text is telling us, in so many words, is that there is no universal, perfectly "centered" reader because there is no universal, perfectly "centered" ideology: hence no universal text and no universal power effect. The universal reader, an ultimate oxymoron in Burke's theory, would need to read nothing. If we can imagine a community of such readers endowed with a single, monolithic ideology, then we can imagine that the need for rhetoric would disappear, and, with it, the expression and application of the power that creates, enhances, and reinforces the ideological subject. For we would all, already, be there, where textual force would take us; the text wouldn't need to make anything happen. It would already have happened. In the land of heart's desire, where will in collective or individual form is no longer set against will, hegemonic political enforcement is superfluous. There, literature may disengage itself from what we know as politics, since politics and rhetoric will surely be unemployed. There, and only there, literature may become a thing unto itself because the social functions that Burke imagines for it will be irrelevant. Literature may then properly become a textual museum, a realm occupied by what eighteenth century theorists called "beauties." There, reading will properly go on as a leisure class activity.

3

In what he calls his "Program," Burke shows his own political preferences most openly, for it is here that his bias for rejectionist aesthetic is stated, and here that he attempts to translate rejectionist aesthetic into oppositional practice. If rejectionist aesthetic could move outside its self-imposed isolation via the mediation of a properly aligned critical intelligence, if it could act effectively in the practical world, if it were to prevail, what would the social structure become? Burke's answer to this question in *Counter-Statement* pushes him in the direction of what I must call the social projection of literary anarchy. It is a theory directed against the devils of anarchy: system and authority. Burke is pleased to call any government "fascist" that prizes such values and the life they demand of efficiency, prosperity, material consumption, "new needs," expansion, and so on. His aesthetic antidote is in keeping with the rejectionist attitude: "inefficiency, indolence, dissipation, vacillation, mockery, distrust, 'hypochondria,' nonconformity, bad sportsmanship. . . ."[28] It will not do to charge him with inadvertently enthroning the values of capitalism by establishing the counter-values of the aesthetic through a process of negation. Burke knows that. He calls his program "negativism" and grants that, so specified, it will have few defenders.[29] But his anarchist distrust of organization, of a "positive" program, is too great to allow him much else. So he pushes oppositional practice in negativist terms to see if there can be any true critical values emerging from such an unlikely source, to see if pure negativity can possibly trigger social change in directions not "fascist." Let us watch him probe the quality of indolence.

> Indolent school children. Beating did little good. They remained indolent. Then it was found that by improving the ventilation one made them less indolent. After which it was found that under a changed curriculum and new methods of instruction many of these school children not only ceased to be indolent but showed an exceptionally keen interest in their studies. So a pandemic of indolent school children might indicate that something is wrong with the school? And the most receptive children might be the ones most depressed by a faulty system? Then might indolence, under certain conditions, be symptomatic of virtue in the indolent? Such is the roundabout defense for the aesthetic side of the conflict.[30]

"Indolent school children"—one of Burke's most condensed and resonant figures, a bridging figure, in fact, that connects his theories of literature and society. And the school system, a key hegemonic site, as synecdoche of the entire sociopolitical structure in dominance: indolent school children, then, as political subjects of opposition who, in their refusal to work, produce, take direction, or become efficient and useful citizens, in turn figure forth the modernist artist whose childish refusals are well known; indolent school children, then, as figures of the oppositional modernist working, not outside, but within the given social space, in the critical mode, as a mover of change. Burke's brilliantly dialectical social allegory of critical consciousness traces the movement whereby apparent sheer negativity passes by imperceptible degrees into a positive attitude and whereby anarchy shades into a program for social change. In a world of wills, there can only be action, never an absence of effect. Burke's negativist ("the man who thinks of power as something to be 'fought' has no hope in perfection—as the 'opposition,' his nearest approach to a doctrine is the doctrine of interference") in fact bears a type of power, what Burke is pleased to call "democracy," facism's proper antagonist: "organized distrust, 'protest made easy,' a Babel of discordant voices, a colossal getting in one's own way—democracy, now endangered by the apostles of hope who would attack it for its 'inefficiency,' whereas inefficiency is the one thing it has in its favor."[31]

This is the inevitable question: How are we to put together, in a coherent theory, the socialist implications of Burke's fable of indolent school children with the radically individualist/anarchist/Emersonian impulse of his version of democracy, a celebration of the antiprogrammatic, isolated, self-reliant, discordant voice that refuses to enter into the chorus of collectivity? Burke will lean decidedly left in another section of the "Program" because he is concerned with the suffering that his discordant anarchist will have to countenance in the name of inefficiency and self-reliance. He will argue, in fact, that a chief political and economic implication of his aesthetic is the redistribution of wealth. But the conflict remains. The point, I think, is not to underscore his contradiction (easy thing to do), for this particular contradiction surfaces only when the literary mind of modernist bent is willing to push itself to its social and political consequences. The point is that for the debilitated literary mind now fully in retreat and sunk in crisis, Burke stands as a rare example of intellectual health—vigorously committed, always engaging the projects of aesthetics with the more significant project for living.

1931 saw the appearance in the United States of two important works of critical theory, in both broader and narrower senses of the term. One of these books has been my subject; the other, which bears striking resemblances to it, and is much more famous, is Edmund Wilson's magnificently conceived and executed *Axel's Castle*. The much more than literary ground covered by Wilson and Burke is almost coincidental, and like Burke's, Wilson's perspective is constituted by political ideals of radical character. The two theorists agree that imaginative writing, from

French symbolism through the big books of English and American modernism, wanted to drop out and almost succeeded in doing so; this agreement forms the common core of their critique. Their differences, which are considerable, subtle, and politically crucial, are best gotten at in a comparison of Wilson's provocative last chapter with what we have seen as Burke's presiding contentions about the ineradicable politics of writing.

For Wilson the alternatives within the symbolist movement are dramatic: *either* Axel—angelist and gnostic, denier of all things living, including his beloved's body, connoisseur of solitary vision, archetype of all symbolist heroes in his icy indifference to society—*or* Rimbaud, antiliterary, literary hero who, in Wilson's sardonic phrasing, finally rejected the life of symbolist writers, those "patient molluscs" excreting "irridescent shells of literature." Rimbaud says in perfect contempt, "I don't do anything with that anymore." For the symbolist the choice was writing or action, and Rimbaud chose action. In Wilson's admiring summary: "if actions can be compared with writings, Rimbaud's life seems more satisfactory than the works of his symbolist contemporaries, than those even of most of his symbolist successors, who stayed home and stuck to literature." Wilson's anger at the symbolist retreat to the frozen poles of imagination is attractive and bracing for most of us, I would guess, but it is also misleading. If Axel and Rimbaud are the only alternatives (let us note that Wilson poises a fictional against a real human being), then we should endorse Wilson's choice.[32]

But not even Wilson can be comfortable with the alternatives, and in his discomfort we find implicated his most significant and problematic political point. Symbolists, he writes, "discourage their readers, not only with politics, but with action of any kind." In the end, the symbolist movement has to be regarded as an aberration of Romanticism: "even Coleridge has more politics than Proust." Wilson is convinced, however, that modern society is not destined to drive the individual ever more deeply inward, in solipsistic revery. With breathless expectation (the year is 1931) he glances toward Russia, "a country where a central social-political idealism has been able to use and to inspire the artist as well as the engineer." What emerges from the last pages of Wilson's book is the typical, cramped, and finally reactionary vision of a thirties Marxist whose patience is heavily taxed by literature that swerves too much from the norms of social realism. (Compare Burke's taste for the avant-garde and his production of the same in his own fiction.) Though preferring Rimbaud's action to the writing that produces a Count Axel, Wilson's true preference is to reject both Rimbaud and Axel, for Rimbaud is ultimately Axel's specular negative—his darkest desire. In Wilson's political universe, Axel stands for the impulse to bad (escapist) writing; Rimbaud for nonwriting. Wilson wants writing, but socially effective writing. He therefore proposes a new literary aesthetic, as a combination of naturalism and symbolism, with naturalism the controlling base and symbolist experiment limited to technique carefully restricted by the demands of what he takes to be a socially responsible content. Underneath this new aesthetic, we can see traditional Marxism's base/superstructure metaphor, refigured as the relationship of naturalism and symbolism; and we can see the traditional aesthetic itself, so easy to align with traditional Marxism, that severs form and content. What we ultimately see is the modernist literary intellectual of activist intention, whose guilty appraisal of his choice of the literary life makes it nearly impossible for him to understand that action and writing can indeed be compared because writing is a type of action. The union of naturalism and symbolism may call forth what Wilson would think a better politics—writing, he thinks, may encourage or discourage such a politics—but he cannot imagine such union as itself political, since for him only a Rimbaud-like gesture of literary rejection for the sake of the "world" can qualify as truly political.[33] In his rhetorical aesthetic, Burke will not separate literary form from political power. For Burke, tough, deviant, avant-garde literature always functions integrally within the unfolding life of a society because it can never really drop out. How integrally, with what kind of force—those are the questions Burke raises and Wilson cannot.

I will conclude with a passage that is closer than any I know to Burke's hopes for the literary intellectual as political force:

> A single book, were it greatly to influence one man in a position of authority, could thus indirectly alter the course of a nation; and similarly the group that turns to "minority" [avant-garde] art may be a "pivotal" group. They need not be pivotal in the sense that they enjoy particular social, political,

or economic prestige—but purely in the sense that they are more articulate and enterprising in the assertion of their views and the communication of their attitudes. Nor must we . . . assume that one cannot be an influence except by "succeeding." The role of opposition is by no means negligible in the shaping of society. The victory of one "principle" in history is usually not the vanquishing, but the partial incorporation, of another.[34]

A superficial reading of this passage will find it naive. In fact, the position extractable from it is cautious, maybe even workable. Now, more than ever, we need to take to heart Burke's linkage of authority, writing, and intellectuals.

Part Four

Start with the crucial Burkean first principle, that all intellection (not excluding the literary sort) is a form of political action, and the first consequence you face is that all intellection is a form of rhetorical activity as well. Rhetoric in turn is the action of a discourse saturated with figures, particularly with metaphor, figure of figures. Metaphor and the other "master tropes," as Burke calls them, must constitute, then, the discursive action of political intention, or, another way of saying the same thing, after Robert Frost, a figure of the will braving alien entanglements: an expression of literary power in a world of powers. The key word for each of these propositions is not "rhetoric," "trope," "power," not even "politics." The key word is "action."

Since the advent of modern culture in the Renaissance, "action" tends to be taken as both the expression and possession of an autonomous agent, and the expressive model most familiar to Western poetics and philosophy (Nietzsche and Heidegger have trenchantly critiqued it) is one of a perfectly self-possessed and therefore lucid human subject who "exteriorizes" something buried within his (not her) "interior." "Action" is (should be)

113

synonymous with rational consciousness—wherever action is rational consciousness must be, because by our actions we inaugurate, govern, and sustain our "republic." And since the meaning of the term "action" hinges on a radically originating, creative function (Burke and de Man agree on this), the active subject must be the radical source of its acts, if the act is to be located in and identified with the subject in question and if (most urgently) the subject is to be held responsible for its acts. Burke has argued forcefully that behind all theories of the act, no matter how secularized, there lies the model of God's creative act: God is ur-model of action, pure origination, pure consciousness, and pure reason—the lucid subject of all subjects. We may argue about whether humans really have an unconscious; we know that God, in order to be God, can't have one. And that is no deprivation, since God can be called the radical source of an originating act only if he has no unconscious. All of which is to say that the divine subject alone is no problem for a theory of action, but the finite human subject definitely is.

From its origin in a slave-holding and sexist society, traditional philosophy conquers the active human subject through a presiding strategy of division and attempted exclusion. (When the classic moves of Plato and Aristotle are actively "passed on"—forcefully handed over, preserved—philosophy becomes "traditional," a form of "tradition-making" and a powerful instrument of the political process.) In the history of Western philosophy, self-possession, lucidity, and reason are persistently aligned with philosophy itself, of course, but also with the male gender. Traditional philosophy since Plato would force us to conclude that the rational subject is necessarily male, that God is too, and that poetry is irrational and womanish. This powerfully influential model of thought (phallic presuppositions are hard to resist) would also force us to conclude that women, however poetic, are incapable of rational action; they can only be acted upon. And if women cannot "act" rationally, then according to the logic of Western culture they are worthless as rhetoricopolitical forces. By in effect "deconstructing" the female subject, by showing it to be itself thoroughly "subjected," its agency always undermined by feeling, traditional philosophy would protect the lucidity and rationality of the male subject; it would keep the agency of the male perfectly integrated with its own agency: traditional philosophy would in this way preserve the integrity of male agency as the undeconstructible, rational source of "free" action.

Although to my knowledge Burke writes no overt feminist theory, his dismantling of the traditional conception of the subject, in that passage in his *Grammar* on the "motivation of an act," strikes at the very intellectual center of the traditional sexist theory of action. His revised conception of the subject shows that the actor (he makes no distinction of gender) is but the agent of action, by no means its origin. Since there are always origins behind origins, what is "active" can always be shown, at another level of analysis, to be "passive": there is no univocal origin. All action is overdetermined. What Burke thus would deliver is nothing less than a mortal blow aimed at the philosophical foundation of the masculine/feminine binary opposition whose political effects are so far-reaching. If the subject cannot be identical with itself, which is the point of Burke's analysis, it cannot be exclusively either masculine or feminine. The category of the subject cannot be conceived as possessing monistic sexual identity.

But if Burke's undermining of the traditional monistic subject (a project he shares with the exemplars of contemporary philosophy—Nietzsche, Derrida, and the Yale Derrideans) is an implicit undermining of sexism, must it also be, as de Man has insisted in a series of influential essays, an undermining of action, rhetoric, and politics? The answer is yes if we understand the political action of rhetoric as necessarily originating in the subject as it is traditionally conceived, always under its vigilant, self-conscious control. After de Man's deconstruction of that subject, we must agree that what he says about speech act theory would probably apply to any theory of action grounded on Cartesian and commonsensical views: the mind that thinks it knows what it is doing, does not. Intention, a category long under attack in modern critical theory, seems confounded for good by de Man. But the salient target of de Man's work of the last decade is not speech act theory; it is political action and any philosophy (Marxism would be the chief offender) that insists on the potential efficacy of the fully engaged life. In de Man's analysis, the futility, the self-delusion, and the paralysis of political activity, especially oppositional political activity, would appear to be a foregone conclusion. If we cannot know who we are, sexually or otherwise, or what we are doing, why bother to intervene? The end of the active intellectual, and not only of the Marxist sort, is intervention, but in such a problematic context intervention would constitute the rashest and least reflective activity imaginable. But as Nietzsche thinks, maybe that is something like an ultimate point about action—it is what it is because it is not reflection.[1]

The crisis in Burke's thought is this: on the one hand, he wants to insist on the political power of literary intellectuals; on the other, he seems to take a position with poststructuralists on the agent of action that, if we accept it, would not only allow us to give up one of the more insidious and stubborn forms of sexism but also force us to give up all chance for a healthy political life. In the cunning nihilism of de Man, one of the great strategies of contemporary theory, its defusion of the masterful subject, is linked to an attack on the classical project for rhetoric, to the end of subverting the political life of the intellect (and feminism is nothing if not political). But what we now call the deconstruction of the subject and of rhetoric need not work on behalf of the will to enervation. Before what we call contemporary theory, Burke traveled similar ways and byways. As usual, however, with a difference. In so many words he raises the following urgent question, that will preoccupy me in the pages ahead: To what degree is literary action compromised by its inescapable historicity—its involvement in tradition, in tradition-making, in a canon, in canon-making; its subjection, in other words, to the binding and potentially subverting pressures of historical force that a deconstructive project always uncovers beneath any act? In Burke's thought, quietism is no corollary of deconstruction. We do not ask the question of Burke that de Man's writing will force upon feminists who have gone to school to poststructuralism: What price feminism? Or, more generally, what price the deconstruction of the Cartesian subject?

I think many of us would admit to the attractions of Burke's politicizing of the literary intellectual. His endowment of the literary intellect with authority in the political sphere has to seem compelling, particularly at this moment, with enrollments sinking fast in the humanities, with the function of the humanist intellectual brought increasingly under the gaze of cynicism, and with some of the most influential advocates of advanced criticism among graduate students apparently content with an isolationist view of their own activities as intellectuals. But I don't believe that Burke gives us an easy high. Earlier I characterized his position as workable and cautious—hardly Romantic qualities, but definitely qualities to be treasured by literary intellectuals of political disposition. In the end, I think that we will want to call Burke's position politically powerful. It is so, however, only because he makes things so hard for us.

1

When Ezra Pound directed his contemporaries to "make it new," he was talking poetic revolution, primarily, but like other major modernists, he was also—perhaps at heart—something of a social theorist and critic, and his dictum has that kind of reach as well. The great sociopolitical example that Pound offers is coincidental with his major poetic achievement. His *Cantos* show that "making it new" implies no violent rupture with the past. The *Cantos* are flooded by the past; they may even represent the triumph of the past. Burke, who seems never to have mentioned Pound, in his major books repeatedly articulates connected theories of literary discourse and social identity that also appear to celebrate the triumph of the past. His comments on Baudelaire in *Counter-Statement* speak to this issue. Baudelaire represents for Burke a genuine critical force against bourgeois values, not because he urges a utopian alternative but because he carries a residual Christian culture into the midst of a secular and materialist society. Though finally nostalgic and counter-revolutionary, the critical power of a residual culture can be as useful, to a point, as the critical power that we might locate in a would-be socialist culture. But—and this is the question—can we choose which critical power we will align ourselves with? Can we choose to align ourselves with an emergent rather than a residual culture? With the future, rather than with the past? The choice of the emergent—or, more dramatically yet, of a rupturing culture—is always the choice of the revolutionary. But if that choice is never open to us as such, in any innocent way, what then of revolution?

Let us take Burke's discussion of the artist trying to come to grips with his own society as an entry into the problem of the writer as political intellectual. "The artist, who is seeking to adjust a vocabulary to a situation (stressing such ways of feeling as equip one to cope with the situation) is necessarily sensitive to both the surviving and the emergent factors in the situation."[2] Notice that in the sense in which Burke is here defining the word, "artist" refers to a consciousness essentially historical in orientation—a consciousness of the past not as past but as present and of the future not as some temporality situated on the other side of a chasm separating futurity from the here and now—but as somehow partially embedded in, and emergent from, the present. The "present" that Burke defines is nothing but the intersection of past and future: "The contemporary being an aggregate of survivals and possibilities, the artist wholly awake to the contemporary will embody a mixture of retentions and innovations."[3] What Burke in *Counter-Statement* calls the "contemporary," or the artist's "situation," is the "present," of course, but a present not present to itself. As an aggregate of survivals and possibilities, or retentions and innovations, presence (that which is present) cannot as such be said to exist. Several decades after Burke made this plea for the radical historicity of the "present," Jacques Derrida, in the semiotic key most comfortable for contemporary theoreticians, defined the presentness of the linguistic sign in similar historical fashion as a crossed structure of retentions and protentions.[4] The point, whether we come at it through Burke or Derrida, is that the writer is most historical not when he tries to make some calculated leap into the past *as such*, in an effort to reach a discourse alien to the present, but when he attends most assiduously to his problematic "present" in its fissured sociolinguistic "immediacy." (It is out of some such sense of history that Burke could give us the linguistically palpable Thomism of Darwin's *Origin of Species*.) The past *as past* is at best an abstraction: a speculative image, formed in the speculative moment, which may or may not interest us but which can never, as a wholly antecedent and completed entity, provide the ground of action because the time of action is always the present. Similarly, the future *as future*, as a temporality not emergent but ruptured from the present, is the product of a purely contemplative process of intellection, in fantastic revery, artificially separated from praxis.

In its clean severance from the present, the autonomous future cannot any more than the autonomous past bring pressure to bear on the present moment as a critical alternative. Such a future is too remote to be touched by our will.

The present properly conceived, therefore, is the time of praxis, but understood in its usual fashion the "present" is inhospitable to action. Praxis taking place in a moment really segregated from past and future, a contemporaneity isolated unto itself, wholly self-present, would in its ahistorical character possess no critical memory of our society's genealogy. It could not reach back—nor would it be able to bring to the moment, in its consciousness blanketed by a temporality utterly immediate, any sense of potentiality, of the possible, of change. It could not stretch forward: any possibility, any protention, any innovation could be meditated only as an impotent object of fantasy in a present totally here—a present so understood (Sartre called it "en soi") is not human time. Action, if we can imagine it in such an arena, would be without point since, so uninformed from both ends, as it were, it could only repeat and thereby reinforce the present in all its presentness. To be without a proper sense of history is necessarily to be complicit with all that is, with the institutions and authorities in dominance; it is to be, willing or not, an agent of the status quo. Burke likes to sharpen the paradox that to be without a sense of history is not only to be without a sense of where we are but also to be disqualified as agents of change.

But the real problem for Burke's artist-intellectual is not how to get a sense of history—Burke after all defines him as the historical consciousness par excellence. The real problem is how not to be overburdened by the pressures of residual cultures and their traditions: how not to be so positioned that our choices are always already made for us. The real problem, as the example of de Man should show, is not how to avoid being a sentimental revolutionary (those of us trained in the history of our disciplines will appreciate this) but how to avoid being professionally constituted a conservative. "Again, since the artist's medium is composed of 'survivals,' being simply his few additions to a long line, his sensitiveness to many cultural values of the past will generally be greater than that of the masses whose own cultural survivals lead them to resist his 'innovations.' That is, the man who has indirectly had Elizabethan values made vivid for him (though approaching them as method, he gets a deeper sense of the attitudes behind the method) will probably endow his 'survivals' with greater vitality than a person in whom they survive mainly because they have not yet been eradicated."[5] Not only is the artist, by virtue of being an artist, inevitably "historical" in Burke's sense of that word; not only will he bring his complicated sense of the historicity of an intersected present to bear in his writing—but his very writing, by virtue of being what it is, by participating in a slower, a literary temporality (a "tradition") that will tend to lag behind economic time, this writing will work as one of the chief constitutive factors of the historicity of the present.

The temporal disjunction of literary tradition and the economic order of things, as Burke understood before Althusser tried to take the measure of a non-Hegelian, heterogeneous, and decentralized social whole, produces several related complex effects. Here, from *Attitudes Toward History*, is Burke's meditation on some fundamental perspectives of *The German Ideology*:

> A given material order of production and distribution gives rise to a corresponding set of manners. (In other words, insofar as the productive pattern attains fixity, it engenders fixed habits, typical occupations, stock situations, and moral evaluations in keeping. These are all summed up, in human material, as manners.) The equivalent of these manners in poetry is *style*. Style is the ritualistic projection or completion of manners. . . . As the productive order changes, manners must adapt themselves accordingly. (We have already noted how long it took to reshape feudalistic manners for the needs of capitalism.) But by the time the need for this reshaping of manners has risen, a whole tradition of "good style" has evolved and been "bureaucratized" (its embodiment giving new writers the "cues" that induce them to perpetuate standards). Writers suffer impoverishments of "alienation" insofar as they attempt to retain and cultivate these purely traditional values of style, "projecting" from one literary heir to the next, while the productive order that gave rise to them has been radically altered, and a corresponding code of new manners has "slid out from in under" the traditional style.[6]

What is remarkable about this meditation on Marx is certainly not Burke's apparent acceptance of the orthodox version of base/

superstructural relations. In effect, his acceptance of the orthodox model becomes strategic, the occasion to work through some
unorthodox manipulations of the model. In this passage he
elides, as he does not elsewhere, the active cultural role of intellectuals in the formation of "manners" and "style" that will
"consent" to the ruling productive order—Burke speaks here
somewhat mysteriously, in passive terms and with no attention
to mediations, of the productive order "engendering" manners.
But his real interest in the passage I've quoted is not Gramscian at
all. His interest is not in where and how consenting consciousness takes shape but in the inevitable temporal dissymmetry of
manners and economic base. This disjunction, or lag, produces
an effect of alienation not accounted for in Marx's manuscripts of
1844. It is not only, in other words, that the means of production
are alienated from the working class. As far as I know, Burke
never disputes that classic Marxist point. He wants, rather, to
enlarge Marx's scope (like critical theorists of the Frankfurt
school) in order to explore alienation at levels other than economic, specifically at cultural levels, and among groups (like
writers) who cannot often be easily aligned with the working
class. His emphasis, again, is on the power of the residual. If
manners, in the large sense that Lionel Trilling would later articulate powerfully in a famous essay (the hum and buzz of a culture:
our patterns of behavior, gestures, our common sense, our moral
judgments as they are visibly and casually embedded in the
quotidian of our work-a-day postures and attitudes)—if all of this
is in a subtle fashion at odds with, alienated from, the economic
structure and the habits it would engender because it takes even
more "time" to reshape consciousness than to reshape the means
and forces of production—then the writer who projects, com-
pletes, and crystallizes those manners in a literary style will lag
even further behind. His solidarity will tend to be with other
writers, especially dead ones. The problem is with the apparent
"semi-autonomy" of culture.

The historical position of the writer is what is at issue here;
what is at stake is writing's historical engagement and potential
political force. Althusser can help us to grasp Burke's point more
securely by showing us, in effect, what it is not. The extent and
force of literature's work in history cannot be measured by the
Hegelian theory that underwrites, in Anglo-American thought,
and via the model of Taine's introduction to his *History of English*

Literature, more theories of literary history than we would ordinarily imagine. For the Hegelian totality is "expressive," as Althusser puts it, a "totality all of whose parts are so many *'total parts,'* each expressing the others, and each expressing the social totality that contains them, because each in itself contains in the immediate form of its expression the essence of the totality itself."[7] In the Hegelian model, writing would be temporally synchronized with the social totality because it would be one of its several perfect expressions. The structural alternative offered by Althusser and prefigured in Burke is not a historical nontotality, no simple negation of Hegel or pluralization of his unified History into dispersed histories, but—tough paradox—a detotalized totality, one in which no single part could function, as in the Hegelian organicist vision, as synecdoche for the whole. Althusser also distinguishes his detotalized structural whole from mechanistic versions of totality in which an economic base works from the outside, as it were, as monolithic cause to determine all superstructural phenomena.[8] In the economist model, writing would be a simple reflection of the economic base with which it would be temporally synchronized.

There is no ontological anchor for the social whole. Rather, there is for Althusser structural determination by the "mode of production," the troublesome "determination in the last instance," which is not, however, determination by an empirically discernible economic base, an external structure, but by a structure that is neither "outside" nor present as expressive substance "in" its parts. For Althusser a structure functions synchronically as the "system of social relationships as a whole," in Jameson's words; but it is nowhere offered by Althusser as anything more than indispensible methodological precondition, a basis for intelligibility, the sine qua non for coherent Marxist interpretation.[9] The stress of both Burke and Althusser is not on the metaphysical temptation of the "last instance" but on semi-autonomous levels, each possessing its own structural and internal necessity and constituting a kind of metonymy, both a "different" and a "differential" history—a history (say, of the literary) whose interest lies in its distinction but whose distinction can only be measured in its lagging "difference" (a relational concept in Saussure's sense) from other histories.[10] The historian's effort must be not merely to note and isolate difference, as is the case with the various formalisms, as if the levels were truly autonomous, but to think difference through mediations to the contexts (any and all other levels) that define it by *their* difference. The notion of semi-autonomy in Althusser demands, as our interpretive goal, that we integrate as much as we segregate.

2

When I refer to "the writer" and "writing" in Burke, I allude to historical conceptions that he criticizes, to the producer of that curiously out-of-step, "traditional" discourse, to the specialized conception of literature that took strong hold in the later eighteenth century, to "imaginative" writing situated in the "mainstream" of a great "tradition" of literature in the reduced modern sense of the word "literature." Raymond Williams's social history of the word "literature" will bear some reiteration and elaboration at this point. Williams traces the term from its fourteenth- and fifteenth-century senses (the condition of being broadly read—"having" literature, *litterae humaniores*—in all manner of writings) to a crucial shift in the later Renaissance and earlier eighteenth century (the objects of such a broad-ranging reader: the whole body of books and writing) to its modernist sense, dating from the basic assumptions of Romanticism: not merely humane learning and writing but imaginative writing that earns its distinction by attempting to empty itself of historical, scientific, and generally utilitarian values. "Literature" in our sense rises to value by a process of negation, by excluding from its domain all "interests," a good Kantian word that indexes the modernist sense of the literary as a general revulsion of the aesthetic from the torpid world of the bourgeoisie and the normalizing perspectives of capitalism. The modernist idea of literature would—for reasons with which we can sympathize, if not accept—thus break free from the integrated, culturally and socially involved idea of the literary that dominated European theories of poetry from Aristotle to Samuel Johnson. In its latest phase, the most specialized contemporary sense that we disseminate in our literary departments, "literature" refers not only to the "imaginative" but to the "great" works of imaginative writing, other types of imaginative writing that are deemed to have fallen short of such a standard being relegated to "minor" or "popular" categories. By redefining "literature" rhetorically, Burke would recapture for the word something like its earlier activist, involved, and comprehensive social reach: literature as the cultural work of words. Nevertheless, the modern working writer, however conceived, is necessarily caught up in the complicated process of history that Althusser describes in *Reading Capital* and Burke himself describes in *Attitudes Toward History*. As an inheritor of Romanticism, the writer will be moved deeply by a desire to enter the canon of great writing, of original geniuses, that we sustain and promote in our classrooms; he will want to be "mainstream" (an important metaphor for traditionalists), to become a citizen of literature's empire.[11]

Such desire forces a methodological and ideological commitment (the values implied by the method) to a "tradition" that Burke, like Raymond Williams, but before Raymond Williams, understands as *traditio*, or traducing, and like Harold Bloom, but before Harold Bloom, understands as producing an overriding sense of belatedness, an anxiety of influence. The huge and relentless projective force of tradition, which is not a "handing over" but a forcing down from "one literary heir to the next," as Burke puts it, tends not only to undercut the chances of "making it new," the modernist ideal of innovative writing, in both literary and social senses of "making it new," but also to create that special modernist alienation called "literary autonomy": an autonomy understood now not as the central, socially innocent category of the various formalisms but as an effect of what I have been describing through Burke and Althusser as the complex temporality of sociohistorical process. We need Althusser again at this point; "literature" in its modernist conception (our ruling conception) achieves its autonomy (really a semi-autonomy) because it is always involved in its own structured literary history. Such involvement produces the lagging, alienated position of the writer in a society (Baudelaire is Burke's exemplary instance) that he desires to engage and to criticize from without.

"Tradition" must never, then, be understood as an entity, a static thing, or a completed process. All locutions concerning "the tradition" should be seen as techniques of psychic defense against our own complicity: our involvement in the creation and diffusion of secular myths like, say, a transcendental realm of purely human truths that the sensitive and the civilized receive in wise passiveness. Tradition is always a willful and open process; tradition is always tradition-making, and as such it deploys three temporal modes: it is necessarily *past*-oriented, though never in its most vital sense an object of antiquarian interests; it is at the same time acutely conscious of a *present* that needs to be controlled by a vision of the past; and, last, in ironic generosity, it bestows a legacy by projecting and in part engendering a *future* similarly dominated. Tradition-making stipulates choices for us now and for those who will come after us. It is we who sustain, disseminate, and enhance tradition, and by so doing we ensure that its projective force, like the proverbial rolling snowball, will be that much harder for our progeny to resist. Tradition-making is a process of historical repression engineered not by the dead but by the living, for the living and for those who shall live. Tradition, to reverse a slogan of Derrida, is always already a present and a future.

The bluntest way to restate the related issues of literary engagement—the "act" of the literary intellectual—and traditional literary temporality, with all their attendant, corrosive ironies, is to say that all writing, but especially the self-consciously literary sort, with its overdeveloped sense of ancestry, has a marked dispostion to suppress its material conditions. In its most usual conception, tradition is a process of ideal, continuous texts, whose ideality and continuity (they are the same thing) are rooted in the absence of roots or, more precisely, in the desire for the absence of roots.[12] Traditional intellectuals, in an active reading often not comprehended as such, produce this deluded and deluding sense of tradition and themselves as detached from social classes and sociohistorical conditions; most "great books" courses and sophomore surveys of literature express and enforce this conception of intellectuality—as teacher/critic, the traditional intellectual in effect creates the "great" books. The literary intellectual, for example, feels an *esprit de corps* with the activities, however diverse, of literary critics since Aristotle—they are all in disinterested pursuit of that elusive essence, Literature; they are all united by the connective tissue of a common conceptual nomenclature. His identity and function as critic apparently not bound materially by class interests, he would produce a text similarly autonomous and ideal. But if we scratch the surface of Gramsci's traditional intellectual we will find another kind of organic intellectual, highly mediated and unselfconscious of his political function, to be sure—*what* political function?—whose "apolitical" criticism, when not directly appropriated for hegemonic work, has the effect of politically tranquilizing students and readers who take it at face value.

The neo-Marxist critical ideal of Raymond Williams to work out a cultural materialism is problematical, then, not because it is wrong-headed but because of what Burke insists is the very nature of the document that has become "traditional": its tendency to survive as crystallizing style, a codification of ideas and feelings out of sync with material life. The fact that a document has survived and become a part of tradition is always understood passively and hence retrospectively by the traditional intellectuals who produce, select, and constantly reselect what is to be celebrated by the honorific term "tradition." What the traditional intellectual tends to ignore, hide, or be unaware of, is his own active work of tradition-making, which causes ideas to survive through time, to become part of the transhistorical myth he calls "Western Culture and Tradition." Such is the materialist genesis of idealism (in its modern phase, what Marcuse called "affirmative culture") and its central technique of repressing cultural heterogeneity. The continuity of the traditional document can be purchased only at the price of its circumstantial specificity: the more rooted and materialized we insist the document be, the more discontinuous with, and less like, other documents it becomes.

Like the traditional document, the artist will be chosen by tradition-makers. The intellectual as artist is made obsessively conscious of tradition, then, *made* a traditional intellectual, by the unavoidable act of apprenticing himself to a medium whose history has already been traditionally defined. He will not "join" tradition as if it were a simple matter of making a decision. He will find himself inserted into a "mainstream" practice, a method and the values implied by the method, within which the distinctive sociohistorical materiality of writing will tend to be dissolved in a homogeneous environment inhabited by "great" texts and often desired by those who would be serious, important writers. And that desire is not innocent; it is always educated—it is always socially produced, as in the situation of our university writers in residence, or those who hold permanent appointments in literature departments, or those who enroll in their workshops: all, all too often flaunting contempt for the critical and scholarly work of their "unimaginative" colleagues, all the while mainly conforming to the canonical choices and definitions of the Ph.D.s who generate and sustain a tradition of curriculum authors (*auctores*).

"Our universities," on the humanist side in particular, remain, as Ernst Curtius has argued, "an original creation of the Middle Ages."[13] Our modern curriculum authors, long established by a process of canon-formation, extend the tradition, which functions as an empire of timeless human wisdom—I do not use the term "empire" casually—and carry over the old sense of "author" as repository of authenticity and authority, although the magisterial medieval canon (we could call it "cross-disciplinary") has been severely disciplined—in Foucault's double sense—in the modernist narrowing of the medieval *auctores*. Our *auctores* are now "literary" masters of an isolated beauty, no longer of truth and goodness; sources of the image, not of the *eikon* or *imago*, the exemplary figure. In the medieval concept of the author, all canonical texts are equally good, as Curtius put it; all belong to no period, have no history—and differentiation by subject matter is unknown.[14] The disciplined modernist canon, on the other hand, is decidedly literary, and we insist on a minimal, highly rarefied historical periodization whose ideality is quite transparent. Our transcendent giants of the sophomore survey speak only to one another, above the differences of time and society; Milton to Wordworth, Wordsworth to Stevens, and so on. Literary history for us tends to be the interbiography of the integrated, self-possessed great men. (And we should underscore "men.") Or, in Harold Bloom's dark variation, the interbiography of great men who fear for their integration, who know that their self-possession depends on violent strategies of appropriation and misreading.

Curtius himself, with a crucial assist from T. S. Eliot in the startling epilogue of *European Literature and the Latin Middle Ages* (he turns there on the very classicism that he had so eloquently detailed) delivers a modernist revision of the openly hegemonic intentions of medieval tradition-making, a new sense of the tradition grounded on the withdrawal of *auctores* from authority and authenticity, in the juridical, political, and epistemological senses of those terms. Curtius relocates authority and authenticity in a purified aesthetic dimension. The continuity of the literary tradition is a fragile thing, he argues, constantly at the edge of irredeemable fragmentation—sometimes sunk out of sight in "epochs of enervation and barbarization." But on the longest of views—the kind that a Curtius can take—those epochs are overcome: this is history's "consolation and its promise." Nothing can replace the literary heritage: "Not philosophies, techniques, political or economic systems. All these can produce what is good—not what is beautiful." In its literary expression the mind achieves its "perfect freedom" (here is the utopian impulse in Curtius foregrounded by his experience of two devastating world wars), and that expression performs its ultimate function for us, its receivers, as an aid to memory—a memory that we trust will secure our permanence beyond all change. "The literary tradition is the medium by which the European mind preserves its identity through the milleniums." The theoretical authority for Curtius's desperate humanism is Longinus, so marginalized in the medieval period but rescued by Curtius for the job of anti-Aristotelianism: it is Longinus who for Curtius first cut the ties between literature and rhetoric, and literature and mimesis, and who proclaimed the high creative spirit—beyond all politics and economics—and the value of transport or literary ecstasy. For modernists tradition is no warehouse of society's resources and tools but a "House Beautiful," an oasis of culture, as Pater put it, that minds of "all generations are always building together."[15]

Giving us an astounding definition of "essence," Curtius writes: "Much must be forgotten if the essential is to be preserved."[16] In such an admission we understand that both modernist and medieval tradition-making intersect in a single effort to exclude all but a single, continuing voice of the hegemonic classes. This voice is preserved by a doubled process of repression (of other voices) and dematerialization (the linking of the "essential" texts, as Curtius says, across the ages, regardless of their differentiating material circumstances). The aesthetic tradition of the image and the classical tradition of the *imago* are rooted in political ground. The new author, the truly creative individual, may enter the tradition, the existing ("ideal") order that is complete in itself, only if the individual talent can modify the whole with his contribution and establish a new sense of that whole with his entry. This famous troubling paradox can be resolved if we understand that literary tradition, as one of the historical discourses of a persistent cultural force, is figured by Eliot as an organic process, necessarily modified by the introduction of new organic substance and then reconstituted as organic self-sufficiency with the potentially disruptive individual talent seamlessly internalized within an ideal order. The enduring stability and independence of literary tradition is synecdochal for Curtius and Eliot. What is at stake in the struggle to keep literature secure is the ideality, the autonomy of culture itself—its imperviousness to the barbarizations of politics and history. Pater's "House Beautiful," like the traditions of Curtius and Eliot, is not really open: invitations to this open house are extended only to those whose cultural formation guarantees that, once within, their manners will be beyond reproach.

It is not the younger Eliot of "Tradition and the Individual Talent" but the nostalgic post-World War II sage of *Notes Toward the Definition of Culture* who brings this discussion almost full circle to its medieval point of departure. Tradition transmits culture, and culture is a great deal more than literary. Culture for Eliot rests on the foundation of religion, and European culture, which is the dominant culture of the West, is the incarnation of Christianity; Christianity gives Europe's culture its unity. The evolution of the arts, our conceptions of Roman law, public and private morality, and literary standards—all of this, Eliot argues, we owe to the Christian heritage. But Eliot is a modernist, not a medieval canon-maker. He rigorously segregates the complex substance of what he calls culture from the political and economic structures of European society. Politics is a dirty activity for Eliot—it gave us the war: it disrupted Europe; devastated Germany, Italy, and France; forced people to take sides and become partisans of ideas; it even destroyed—and this he says without a trace of irony—the cultural universalism of his quarterly review, *The Criterion*. In its last years (the late 1930s), Eliot claims *The Criterion* "failed" because it was forced to assume a "point of view." Ideas, properly approached, in their cultural ambiance, within what he calls the "spiritual organism" of Europe, are delighted in "for their own sake, in the free play of intellect." And we note the Arnoldian echo. Improperly approached, ideas become fully functioning weapons within Europe's political or what he calls its "material" organization. Therefore (Pater is hard to escape for a modernist) the entire activity of culture must be spiritualized by Eliot in order to preserve it against worldly contingencies and work in the world.[17]

This is desperate stuff. The unity of European culture is presumably independent of politics but not, Eliot admits, free from the effects of politics. The war brought great material devastation. Can the engines of material devastation reach into the realm of spirit? Can the "spiritual organism" of Europe perish? Theology says that the spirit cannot perish, but Eliot says that "these spiritual possessions are also in imminent peril," and in admitting that he comes close to admitting that the diffusion of culture is part of the will to political power, that "making it prevail," as Arnold put it, is of the essence of the matter, that culture is intimate with the grubby political world of material organization. If the great men of culture "worked powerfully to diffuse sweetness and light," then on Arnold's account Eliot, like his numerous progeny in our literary departments, is certainly no great man. Eliot was merely a coterie modernist poet who refused the Arnoldian mission: he had "no passion for diffusing . . . for carrying from one end of society to the other"; he did not labor "to divest knowledge of all that was harsh . . . difficult, abstract, professional, exclusive"; he did not "make it efficient outside the clique of the cultivated and learned."[18]

In these failures Eliot is not alone. His definition of culture, though heavily mediated by his sense of Christian tradition, does not rest on medieval social ground—its true subtext is bourgeois society, and it may ultimately even bear, against all his obvious intentions, the tragic vision of the bourgeoisie. His idea of culture is full of the pathos of what Marcuse called "affirmative culture": the dominant "culture of the bourgeois epoch which led in the course of its own development to the segregation from civilization of the mental and spiritual world as an independent realm of value . . . . Its decisive characteristic is the assertion of a universally obligatory, eternally better world . . . a world essentially different from the factual world of the daily struggle for existence, yet realizable by every individual for himself 'from within' without any transformation of the state of fact."[19] "Culture" is affirmed, in short, because it is where we are free and equal; culture is affirmed, then, not mainly in order to saturate society with the idealized interests of a powerful class—Eliot is finally no Arnoldian—but because in his view bourgeois society is a realm of actual unfreedom for the individual, as opposed to the abstract idea of freedom that is our central myth. This society must be denied by culture.

Against Curtius, Pater, and Eliot, I am arguing that the so-called Longinian tradition of the beautiful, like the Aristotelian/Horatian tradition of empire it would replace, bears a humanist vision projected by a socially dominant class. Our humanism is different from the earlier humanism detailed in Curtius's book in that it is dedicated to the alienated proposition, grounded on the bourgeois malaise of Curtius's German idealist forebears, that only the aesthetic can make us free. Earlier humanists were more candidly imperialistic in the literal sense, as Frank Kermode has shown us in *The Classic*, more openly political in their sense of their own activities. They did not stake *their* freedom on poetry. Nevertheless, as Curtius admits in all but words, the price of freedom for some is its denial to others. We purchase and preserve our identity beyond all change with the currency of a will to power rooted in an ethnocentric idea of community (the "European mind" celebrated by Curtius and Eliot) that would exclude and silence the voices in conflict with it. The human costs of the rhetorical action of tradition-making are grim, and the mere pluralization of voices and traditions (a currently fashionable and sentimental gesture) is inadequate to the ultimate problem of linking repressed and master voices as the agon of history, their abiding relation of class conflict. Tradition-making functions precisely to hide class conflict by eliding the text's involvement in social struggle. The judgment of Aulus Gellius, a second-century canon-maker who seems to have been the first to have used the term "classic" in the sense of "traditional text," has itself acquired traditional power: "*Classicus . . . scriptor, non proletarius.*"[20] The modern view of the canonical texts and the imperialist view of the Middle Ages may be closer than either Curtius or Kermode think. And for all the welcome trouble that the new Yale critics and their followers have injected into the moldy traditionalist academy, the latest avant-garde has pretty much endorsed the traditional canon.

3

There is a certain ambiguity in the term "writer" as it appears in my discussions of Burke and those Western Marxists like Gramsci, Marcuse, and Williams with whom I would associate him. These theorists want to believe in the possibility of writing as critical action in the world, and to varying degrees they give just such political weight to the term, both in their conception of the intellectual as writer and, most concretely, in their own work as writers. On the other hand, the "writer" they conceive in radical fashion is necessarily caught up in that many-tentacled process of normalization that I've been calling tradition-making. This big cultural process and its specific strategy of canon-formation would subvert, as conservative action, the critical impulse of writing: that is the basic political motive of tradition-making and canon-formation. Make it "normal," or, when that fails, declare it "deviant" (without value). Foucault has given us an important analysis of the social force of normalization at work in the disciplinary activities of modern capitalist society's institutions. I want now to contextualize the theory and application of normalization in Foucault's work, where it is coincidental with the emergence of modern society, by examining normalization within the classical mimetic mode. This larger context, this longer history of the process of normalization, will give us a daunting perspective on how difficult it is to achieve the literary action that Burke has in mind. Yet classical normalization by no means rests on a settled, monolithic foundation, as is so often claimed by both its defenders and its detractors. To the end of unsettling our normal views of that most normalizing of traditions, classicism itself, I will offer a highly schematic reading that will focus on certain faults in the foundation that may function as traces of a critical enemy within.

Alexander Pope's "Essay on Criticism" may stand as one of our best works on the subject. The origin of tradition, as well as of its canonical texts, is what Aristotle called the object of imitation—"At once the source and end, and test of Art." Pope calls the object to be mirrored Nature: "One clear, unchang'd, and universal light." He means by "nature" something very like the substance and ground of reason's authority—normative in force, permanent, above the tamperings of time and the will: the law at once of humane living and art, but not itself a human invention ("Those Rules of old discovered, not devis'd"). But in his humanist celebration Pope is more candid than our academic humanists. Nature's original, objective, and transcendent authority is never encountered in anything but books: sacred, juridical, literary. Imitations cannot be checked against their objects; the precepts were drawn by the ancients, in Pope's words, from the "great examples given": in other words, from *their* texts, not from the source itself. I would thus urge a different reading of one of Pope's most well-known lines. "Nature and Homer are the same" not because they stand as mirror images of one another, in a relationship of perfect adequation, but because nature is always and only encountered in the Homeric encoding—as Virgil learned to his amazement and horror.[21]

In the closing lines of "An Essay on Criticism," Pope reveals the objectivity of nature for what it is: a useful fiction for tradition-makers and empire builders, an epistemological appeal that would hide the human power which engenders the fiction of objective nature in the drive to establish, found, and disseminate both tradition and empire. Can nature fall? Learning and Rome certainly can—when the "barbarians" they create and then exclude seize the day:

> Learning and Rome alike in empire grew,
> And arts still followed where her eagles flew;
> From the same foes, at last, both felt their doom,
> And the same age saw learning fall, and Rome.[22]

Pope's brutal linkage of power, learning, and politics at the end of the poem deserves to be contrasted with the more sanguine, and I think deceptive, assessment that he delivers at the close of Part I. His naturalization here of tradition as a "stream" ever burgeoning in its flow through time is the figure that subsumes most humanist considerations of tradition-making. Tradition, in this view, is safe from all ignoble human activities:

> Secure from flames, from envy's fiercer rage,
> Destructive wars, and all-involving age.
> . . . .
> Hail bards triumphant! Born in happier days;
> Immortal heirs of universal praise!
> Whose honors with increase of ages grow,
> As streams roll down, enlarging as they flow.[23]

The paradigm for these key strategies of tradition-making in the great mimetic mode lies in Horace's *Epistle to the Pisos*, which opens innocently enough with some observations about the natural world. "If a painter chose to set a human head on the neck of a horse, to gather limbs from every animal and clothe them with feathers from every kind of bird, and make what at the top was a beautiful woman have ugly ending in a black fishes tail": he goes on in this fashion, and we very quickly get the point—the norms of nature would render such imitations absurd. And the fact that many of us have cultivated a taste for aesthetic representation in the visionary and surrealistic styles generally does not negate but, rather, underscores Horace's point. Our appreciation is based on our keen awareness of the difference of nature's norms from the aesthetic norms of Blake or Dali. The opening of Horace's *Epistle* is cleverly calculated. Once he has us hooked, he can go on and "root" in natural ("genealogical") ground a desired purity and hierarchy of the various "genres," a typology for character representation, a concept of literary transmission ("do ye thumb well by night and day Greek models"), and even an ideal of common sense. This naturalization of literary culture and its epistemic authorization can work only if it rests on the prior naturalization of society itself: literary character types are based on social types, which "come from" natural types. Deviations (we need its strong sense) from the literary order of things and from the social order are deviations from nature itself. Such, I think, is the "genesis" and range of the classical notion of "decorum"—a term whose literary sense of

formal integrity must not obscure its mimetic function, the supposed fitness of literary, social, and natural structures.[24]

At the other end of classicism, Sir Joshua Reynolds's third
discourse opens, like Horace's *Epistle,* with observations that are
difficult to resist. Mere imitation of actual objects is no good. The
young painter must cultivate an abstracting kind of perception,
imitating a structure shared by many particular objects but incar-
nated perfectly by no one of them. Such mimesis is not copying
but the creation of some "central form." Reynolds goes on for a
number of paragraphs in this way—and he is persuasive because
all his examples have to do with the representation of the physical universe. We could argue with him about the ontology of
what he and Samuel Johnson call "general nature," or we could
argue about the desirability of basing an aesthetic on such a
conception (whatever the ontology); but we see what they mean,
and in some contexts we go along with it. But if we go all the way
with Reynolds (or with Horace), we will have to accept his ideology of the type. Like Horace, Reynolds moves from a meditation
on nature to social types, then to an implied ranking of the
literary genres (recalling the conservative neo-Aristotelians from
Castelvetro to Dennis and Rymer) that assumes a naturalized
class structure, and finally to an ideal of literary value and staying
power ("you will please posterity") that assumes such naturalizations. The classical mind projects a continuity of the literary
tradition that simply requires naturalization—and the freezing
for eternity of a hierarchical social order. The point is not that
types should (or can) be avoided but that they are socially produced and that the order of social production is always in process, not crystallized and frozen. By hiding its work of social
production in "what goes without saying," classicism masks the
political work of its literary theory.[25]

Between Horace and Reynolds stands Castelvetro's discussion
of the persons proper to tragedy and comedy. It is an especially
resonant discussion in this context, because it stands as a naked
rationalization of the social order in dominance. His focus on the
relation of high and low characters to the law suggests the most
cynical perspective on political power, softened only by an attitude of *contemptus mundi* and its correlative posture of humility.
However sincerely felt by Castelvetro himself, *contemptus mundi*
functions in his commentary on Aristotle (and for his contempo-

rary Antonio Minturno, as well as for all heavily Christianized reading of Aristotelian catharsis) as a vehicle of social control. The royal persons of tragedy, who have "greater souls," are images of arrogant power. They are unchecked: "they do not run to the magistrates to make complaint of . . . injury nor do they bear it patiently, but they make a law for themselves." The persons of comedy, on the other hand, "are of poor spirit and inclined to obey the magistrates and to live under the laws and to endure injuries and damage . . . . They do not make laws unto themselves." The real problem, as Castelvetro well understood, was to limit the audience for tragedy to those not subject to the rule of others.[26]

The human stresses of social history force themselves even into literary theory: a comparison of Reynolds and Samuel Johnson, beginning perhaps with their different social backgrounds, becomes a mirror of social change—Reynolds, upholder of all hierarchies, versus Johnson, supposed summation of the neoclassical spirit, who defended Shakespeare against the charge of violating character typology by pointing out that you could find buffoons in the senate; who defended Shakespeare against the charge of violating the decorum of genres by pointing out that in real life social distinctions are often overrun because "the high and the low cooperate in the general system by unavoidable concatenation"; and who praised Shakespeare's comedic style because it achieved a middling bourgeois currency—"a common intercourse of life, among those who speak only to be understood, without ambition of elegance . . . a conversation above grossness and below refinement." Let us add that his well-known appeals to reason and nature (beyond what he calls "prejudice" and "the rules") are those of the enlightened man, with little patience for the claims that social privilege and authority make for themselves. In the same "Preface to *Shakespeare*," Johnson contradicts himself on all these points. His contradictions may be textually anchored in the key neoclassic term "general nature" (a term he shares with his friend Reynolds, who uses it univocally), a term that moves in one direction very conservatively, in all senses of that word, toward the neoclassical universal—Pope's nature, Horace's types, Reynolds's hierarchical correlation of painterly and literary genres, and all naturalizations of social hierarchy—and at the same time in another direction, to a "strong equalitarian orientation," in Wimsatt's apt phrasing, "the common audience and their spontaneous vote." I want to urge, though, that we understand this contradiction not merely as an intellectual issue, a personal failure of logic and consistency, or even as a clash of systems in the history of ideas, but as a socially determined contradiction—not an undecidability or an aporia that may be textually enclosed. Johnson's praise of Shakespeare is carried by an emergent bourgeois voice laced with the anger of the outsider; his censure of Shakespeare, on the other hand, proceeds out of ruling class norms and represents, perhaps, the heartbreaking effort of the outsider to make it, to get into the mainstream.[27]

4

Unlike most modernists Kenneth Burke has always understood the political and historical costs of "tradition" and "canon-formation." The cultural and the political are for him, as for classical thinkers, two expressions of a single human economy. Together with his own deconstruction of the act and the active subject, such integrated understanding has always accompanied his romantic call to intellectual practice. Which is to say that his Romanticism is never of the airy sort. To borrow a phrase from F. Scott Fitzgerald, Burke shows us how as writers, whatever our intentions, we are "borne back ceaselessly into the past," into a past dematerialized because of its essentialized, canonical survival. Against our usual views of the interrelated conceptions of the autonomous subject, intention, and personal identity, Burke brings his central proposal of "action" not as the production of an "agent" who would be in turn conceived as the expressive origin and master of "action" but as a transpersonal, all-embracing process within which agents are always already situated. With a magisterial command of intellectual history that we associate with Hegel in the nineteenth century and that we are beginning to associate with Derrida in our own time, Burke moves easily from the pre-Socratics through nineteenth-century anthropological work on animism, to argue that cultural trends emphasizing that "all things are full of Gods" (as Thales thought) would translate, in our more resolutely secularizing vocabularies, into "all things are full of powers" or "motives" that cannot be grounded in agent terms like "personal identity." The collapsing of conceptions of motives, powers, and action into the subject-agent is an effect of what Burke calls a "capitalist psychosis"—the rise of private property as a privileged category of value and the concomitant reconstruction of identity, motives, action, and power as analogues of private property, "possessions" of the subject. But if intention, action, motives, power, and identity are not "properties" of agents, then the rhetorical work of writing as political action is made problematic not only because the writer is drawn back into traditional values against all intention but also because the political act of writing cannot control its own political desire, maybe even cannot know itself fully enough as political action because the overt, conscious act of writing is involved in an unconscious of writing/action whose exposed tip is canon-formation and whose relation to consciousness is therefore disturbingly uncertain. If we can come this far, through these meditations on the historicity of writing and of the "present," and now through this meditation on action—through these potentially paralyzing (de-monic) meditations—then perhaps we are ready to understand in a complicated and sobering sense Burke's calling (against the ominous background of the mimetic tradition) of the literary intellectual to action and the world.[28]

Let me put the question this way: Is it possible for the writer so caught up in tradition and traditional power to *be* a power and, in however modest a fashion, to *make* alternative history? I have emphasized as many reasons as I could locate in Burke and in our literary heritage to say no to this question, not ultimately in order to negate the politics of writing but in order to forestall a prema-ture, overly enthusiastic yes. I turn now to a side of Burke, better known probably than any other, in which the affirmative is foregrounded. I allude to his notion of "symbolic action," and I want at the outset to put aside a potentially debilitating inter-pretation of this idea that would, in stressing its "symbolic" quality, perhaps inadvertently (but perhaps not) negate aesthetic praxis by suggesting that symbolic action is not to be confused with real action. By "symbolic action" Burke means action with very wide-ranging representational force, rooted in the personal (even the biological) but reaching out through the familial into the large structures of society. And literature conceived as symbolic action is not only broadly representational—it is at the same time thoroughly pragmatic. It is what Burke calls "equipment for living."

In this phase of his theory, Burke does not stress his radically deconstructive reading of the motivation of an "act"—the act always behind the act, the motivation always behind the motivation. Rather, he insists that for all its problematic character—for all the necessity of confronting it with a hermeneutic of suspicion, for all the good reasons to conceive the act as always already past, irretrievably fading into a history, an intertext too dense and too complicated really to master, in spite of all of this, with all of this acknowledged and assented to—there remains in the act a wholly urgent hereness: a present and a simultaneous presencing of past and future. The literary act remains an act. Whatever the unknown and uncontrollable forces acting upon and through it, in its manipulation of form the literary act produces force and thereby sets loose effects in the "present" that Burke understands as a temporal crossing. In the act of writing, one of the key cultural sites where past and present are crossed, the present is experienced as history. In the act of writing, then, we may be given dramatic, linguistically palpable access to the opening of the present, which, otherwise conceived as full presence, is the impervious, closed, spatially solidified nightmare of the fascist state horrifically evoked in the recent writings of Foucault.

From the historicity of writing, from its crossed temporal and social status, the lugubrious and paralytic conclusions of deconstruction do not necessarily follow. Witnesses as diverse as Burke, Althusser, Lacan, and de Man agree that the act (a conscious thing) is compromised by a past (an unconscious) that invades it and makes it passive (a nonact). De Man's apparently outrageous contention that we do not and cannot know what we are doing is in some part true and must not be set aside. I doubt that anyone seriously disposed to history could successfully disagree with him on this issue. But the act so deconstructed, to reveal forces within it beyond the consciousness of the active subject, is not the act canceled, called back, and inserted into the fatality of history. The literary act cannot be restrained within an enclosed contemplative space beyond praxis. The lacerating self-contempt of the intellectual, who has been sold an ironic bill of goods called "powerlessness," is not only premature and excessive: it is unnecessary. For there remains in the act an irreducible contemporaneity, which is its temporal ground and the guarantee of its activity, the sanction of its ability to make something happen. This contemporaneity and its consequences permit us to write "act," sometimes, without enclosing the word in quotation marks. So despite its far reaches of hidden passivity, all the activity of the act is not drained off into the past: we must face the disquieting fact of force in our own writing and teaching.

To situate the praxis of the intellectual act in its contemporaneity, without setting aside the shaping force of any act's historical unconscious, is to join the politics of the intellect to the politics of tradition and tradition-making that is always a choosing and a deciding for others. Tradition-makers—I refer especially to humanist intellectuals as writers and teachers—do not escape the ironic subversions of de Man. But above everything else, tradition-makers of this sort should be keenly aware that they are involved in the dissemination of values; they should understand that they are making choices for contemporaries and for the future; that they are profoundly implicated in the enforcement of a politics of sociocultural conservation and continuity. The humanist intellectual is an enforcer who should know what he is doing. To put it another way: a tradition-making imagined as unconscious could produce no well-ordered canonical arrangement of texts and doctrines. The existence of a canon of traditional texts as a persistent, stubborn structure is proof of our conscious collective responsibillity as tradition-makers and canonizers who with remarkable consistency select and exclude within predictable patterns of choice.

Yet the politics of cultural enforcement, which is in some ways thrust upon the tradition-maker who is always belated, never temporally prior, is by no means the whole story. We must not, as it were, take tradition at its own word. As a theory of historical process, tradition would stipulate that its continuity, its power to hand over and hand down, is guaranteed by the ideality of the traditional object necessarily conceived as an essence, a thing forever repeatable that may be accreted with the sediments of different societies and cultures—dispositions, renovations, accommodations, as Kermode calls them—in its movement through time but that is never contaminated in its essential core.[29] In the traditionalist's own strictest account of this process, there is no tradition-making but only tradition-receiving: the traditionalist is a passive agent, never an active participant. The traditionalist's contemporaneity in this account, then, is mainly a biological, rarely a social and cultural force. But the difficult, intersected contemporaneity of the so-called tradition-receiver, his sociocultural locus, is not the site of a veiling appearance through which a reality is viewed. It is not a differentiating circumstance ultimately dissolvable in the permanence of an essence, the process of ideal traditional objects whose identity cannot be compromised by the history through which they move. Neither the literary object nor its receiver exists in that transhistorical community that putatively defines Western civilization (a "general nature" that demands "general readers"). The contemporaneity of the tradition-receiver must be viewed, rather, as the vital site of tradition-making, a ground on which the so-called ideal object is not only received but reconstituted in an active reception which *makes* relevant, *makes* contemporary ("Learning and Rome alike in empire grew"). The difference made in such active reception makes this difference: the reconstitution of the ideal object in the crossed contemporary moment assures the continuing force of the residual while it represents an emergent force, in active conflict with the old, engaging the old in a war of cultural struggle; active reception permits the persistence of the old but only on condition that the needs of the new are satisfied. The contemporaneity of the tradition-maker, in the most active sense of "maker," is the site of historical struggle; active reception is the site where the will of the residual and the will of the emergent interact and clash, the site where, for better or for worse, the cultural future is decided, where differences (and not only linguistic ones) are made. The purpose of the traditionalist's account of tradition, however, is to promote its own inevitability by covering up that struggle. (Kermode's term "accommodation" is helpful in that it points to the active nature of reception; it is deceptive because too soft—it too hides the fact of struggle.) Beneath the pieties of the humanist's tradition—his self-effacing, reverential, and dutiful attitude—lies a will to power, a constant activity of appropriation, carried out in the name of love and of the Father, on behalf of the son's anger and liberation.

There is, then, an irreducible self-consciousness in tradition-making, or at least in some tradition-makers, that may engender some critical distance on the very political process within which we tradition-makers find ourselves enmeshed and which we help to keep going. We may to some important degree both inventory and evaluate the traces history has marked us with, as Gramsci once put it, and we may thereby meditate critically upon our historicity as agents of the past and makers of the future.[30] The political nightmare that deconstructors generate for themselves and others is motivated by a repressive forgetting of such possibility and of their own best slogan: "no historical repetition without difference." In the strong sense of the word "difference," Burke would have us think about our responsibility for those differences, would have us understand that the historical process is not necessarily the story that Foucault tells in *Discipline and Punish* (an ever constricting movement toward carceral dystopia) but a narrative whose future episodes are genuinely open; he would encourage us to understand, against a certain Marxism, that historical process is never teleologically assured. The point is not to step outside tradition—that can't be done; nor is the point to condemn and dismiss the traditional text—that can be done, but isn't worth doing, unless we think it best not to know how we got to be culturally where we are. The point is that the traditional text needs to be historically restored, all traditionalist desire to the contrary notwithstanding: its politically activist, materially textured substance (made well-nigh invisible by the humanist academy) brought to light in an act of reading that penetrates the idealist myths (whether Meyer Abrams's or de Man's) that have veiled the text's real involvement in human struggle.

However hedged by a historicopolitical unconscious, or even, as in Burke's example of Coleridge, by a biological unconscious, the act is in some part irreducibly conscious; we are in some crucial part responsible for what we *are* conscious of. We may never wholly know what we are doing, as de Man argues, but in some part we do, and to that part at least we must hold ourselves to political account. The deconstructive argument—from Marx and Nietzsche through Freud, Saussure, Burke, Derrida, Lacan, and de Man—shows us the many ways in which the master is not the master, but that argument must not be read as a determinist one. Intention and the subject, as Derrida has insisted, are not destroyed; they are situated in a way so complicated as to be almost overwhelmed. But not "overwhelmed"—that is a term for fatalists. Despite the insidious and astonishing historical endurance of the activity of tradition-making (that cultural mechanism that ideologically reproduces social hierarchy and political domination by passing on a dominant culture, a view of what it means to be educated—tradition-making and canon-formation reinforce each other) there remains the historically stubborn story of resistance, whose marks continue to be made within those very mechanisms that reproduce existing, stratified power relations. Resistance cannot be set aside—the voice of the barbarian insists on speaking within those "great books" that would silence its collective implication. Who really is that mad poet Horace imagines at the end of his *Epistle to the Pisos?* Why is this imagined madman then accused as one who has defiled the graves of his ancestors? For whom does he speak? The various theories of social and political reproduction—deconstruction is sometimes one of those theories—tell a compelling but flawed story, for they often help to produce intellectuals in colleges and universities, teachers and students alike, who are nothing but cultural dupes. (Is this the ironic legacy of the traditional academic liberal who has always insisted on the division of cultural and political power?) However morally comforting, the position of the cultural dupe is not one we can sustain with any honesty. Our historical work must be textually more subtle than ever because the ante of political accountability has been raised to a frightening degree.

Part Five

I turn now to Burke's most provocative meditation on the writer as political force—his conceptual center as an intellectual, if it is possible to speak of a centered Burke. The following passage on Nietzsche's style will inform much of what I say on rhetoric, the subject of subjects in Burke.

> Nietzsche's later style is like a sequence of *darts*. Indeed, at first I tried to explain it to myself as a simple conversion of his fighting, hunting attitude into its behavioristic equivalent. His sentences are forever striking out at this or that, exactly like a man in the midst of game, or enemies. They leap with a continual abruptness and sharpness of naming, which seems to suggest nothing so much as those saltations by which cruising animals suddenly leap upon their prey. . . . But however much the state of his mental or neurological structure may account for this dartlike quality of his page, an equally important source of it is revealed in his word "perspective." Nietzsche, we learn in his *Will to Power*, was interested in the establishment of perspectives. It was part of his program to give us these repeatedly. And in trying to analyze just what he meant by them, I came upon reasons for relating his cult of perspectives to his dartlike style.[1]

1

In the scary, ironic discourse of Mafia dons (experts in these matters) the rhetorician is one who persuades us by making us an offer we believe we can't refuse. Persuading can seem friendly (a "friendly persuasion") or otherwise (as with a "persuader"—a gun, a knife, a whip, a piece of piano wire, or a word). In either instance rhetoric is a form of powerful action: darting, killing, drug dispensing, (doctor, pusher, hit-man, poisoner, healer). Each of these metaphors in Burke, with their immense history in rhetorical and literary theory, are figures for an essential process of representation involving teaching and writing in an action, to cite his two key words, of "identification" and "transformation." Burke's extended meditation on rhetoric—though intimately affiliated with the ancient traditions, as current poststructuralist writing on rhetoric is not—still very much shares with Nietzsche and the Yale neo-Nietzscheans the proposition that rhetoric does not sit upon the stabilizing foundation of "dialectic" in the classical Greek sense of that word. Like the darting saltations of Nietzsche's style, we cannot read rhetoric's force back to some logical base and thereby defer rhetoric by referring its linguistic violence to some legitimating source in reason. Rhetoric insists on presenting itself with stunning abruptness and discontinuity. Rhetoric is irreducible. And there is no alternative to it: "Wherever there is persuasion, there is rhetoric. And wherever there is 'meaning,' there is 'persuasion.' "[2]

Keeping in mind what Burke says about Nietzsche's later style, that it is "like a sequence of darts," maybe we should ask ourselves (more pointedly) what is the point of rhetoric? Of the texts that he takes up in the introductory sections of *A Rhetoric of Motives* Burke writes: "Since these texts involve an imagery of killing (as a typical text for today should) we note how, behind the surface, lies a quite different realm that has little to do with such motives. An imagery of killing is but one of many terminologies by which writers can represent the process of change. And while recognizing the sinister implications of a preference for homicidal and suicidal terms, we indicate that the principles of development or transformation ('rebirth') which they stand for are not strictly of such a nature at all."³ The "point" of rhetoric (as persuasion) is to change its intended receivers, and killing one's auditors is certainly one way of changing them. But a terminology of killing is metaphoric for Burke, however literal it may be for underworld theorists of the subject (and their targets). To change or transform the object of rhetoric is the point of rhetoric, it always is. But Burke's metaphor for Nietzsche's stylistic effect of "darting" foregrounds rhetoric's intention to control and to dominate, to pin us to the wall. Moreover, he argues, Nietzsche's darts establish "perspectives"; they are modes of knowledge: not in its traditional, disinterested humanist definition, but knowledge as power. "Perspectives" are like "darts." To write is to know is to dominate. That is maybe too sinister a way of phrasing the rhetorical process. Burke permits us another phrasing. To write is to establish perspective by metaphor, by incongruity ("establish": fix, ordain, found permanently, as in the founding of governments or institutions). To make metaphor is to violate in one act the status quo of discourse and of society (and here Burke retends Marx and protends the Derrida of "White Mythology"). To make metaphor is to violate linguistic "propriety" and the "proper," conceptions which, as Marx insists, are intimately related to private property—mine, my own.⁴ In the rhetoric of metaphor, language asserts its collective, classless potentiality as it moves against a stubborn, constellated series of notions like origin, privacy, ownership, virtue, the bourgeois subject, the liberal individual—all of which undergird the cultural staying power of capitalism. The rhetorical act in its metaphoric phase moves simultaneously against base, "property," and the habits and values, linguistic "manners," aligned with it in the superstructure. And against not just any social formation but, as the terms of Burke, Marx, and Derrida would indicate, in this convergence of theorists, against the dominant social formation in the West today. Burke insists that art conceived as rhetoric opens up radically divergent social functions for the writer. He may work, as in the writer's classical vocation, on behalf of a dominant hegemony by reinforcing habits of thought and feeling that help to sustain ruling power: at the stylistic level this means, among other things, that the writer sustains consensus and the social structure by reinforcing the metaphors of everyday life that are buried in clichés—and clichéd consciousness—by passing on the "truth" of dead metaphors, and naturalized conventions, like "free enterprise."[5] Or he may work counter-hegemonically as a violator, in an effort to dominate and to re-educate (*in*form), to pin us to the wall, in order to assist in the birth of a critical mind by peeling off, one by one, and thus revealing to us for what they are, all bourgeois encrustations of consciousness. In the widest sense of the word, he would encourage cultural revolution.

This latter potentially disruptive, socially critical act of "transformation" does its work with the crucial assistance of a co-conspirator which Burke calls "identification." Transformation and identification are modes of rhetoric's deepest desire: to move from "the state of Babel, after the Fall," toward another "state"— political state and "state" of language—of perfect understanding and community, that recovery of paradise in which rhetoric ceases to have an occupation.[6] Here we find ourselves in the ambiguous dream world of the visionary. No visionary in any active sense, Burke directs his rhetorical theory on behalf of the formation of a critical consciousness whose main work lies today, particularly in the United States, in the exposition of ideological formations of the advanced capitalist sort. Identification may be ultimately, and dangerously, "compensatory to division," as he puts it, but before we get to that place in history there is much undramatic work to be done.[7]

We can begin to get a hold on Burke's politically intriguing use of "identification" if we note a certain ambiguity that he does not bother to specify, much less clarify: identification *of*/identification *with*. "Identification with" operates at the mediating level where Burke situates rhetoric itself. It is conscious, as when we identify ourselves with our occupations; it is also elusively unconscious, and necessarily so under advanced capitalist norms of dispersion that encourage us to think of what we do as autonomous activity. Nevertheless, as Burke notes, the shepherd, though he thinks he works independently, for the good of the sheep, to protect them from harm, is linked to a project that is raising the sheep for market. The shepherd—writer, teacher—who needs to think that he runs his own show, that in his own special corner of culture he does "good," despite all the isolating specialization his act requires to be done "right," is "enrolled" (an important term for Burke) in a larger social action—unconsciously he is aligned rhetorically, he is identified with this larger action, just as he is always enrolled in (identified with), all democratic myths of the Adamic self to the contrary notwithstanding, a class or at least an "interested" socioeconomic "group."[8] To exist socially is to be rhetorically aligned. It is the function of the intellectual as critical rhetor to uncover, bring into the light, and probe all such alignments. That is part of the work of ideological analysis. Only when such political work of identification is understood, when our various and devious "identities" are put on the table, when our involvements are brought thus bluntly before us, in all their repugnant detail: only then can the rhetorical work of transformation realistically begin.

"Identification with" requires that the critical rhetor perform the dangerous act of "identification of": the political work of ideological analysis presumes a power-enabling act of cognition—an identifying that necessarily entails a knowing and a mastering. If one of the marks of rhetoric from ancient times, as Burke notes, "is its use to *gain advantage*, of one sort or another," then his own working through the process of identification and transformation shows unmistakably that gaining advantage is synonymous with taking it.[9] The critical rhetor finds himself at the most delicate of all crossings, standing at a specific institutional site where any intellectual who teaches, whether as teacher in the conventional sense, or as writer, both dreads and longs to be, the place (this has been the burden of my argument) where intellectuals always already are. The dread of such a politically sensitive position has been expressed with maximum force by Foucault in *Discipline and Punish*. Modern society, in his narrative, is the full realization of knowledge-as-power-to-control. All our significant institutions are unified by an all pervasive carceral intentionality from which there is no escape; the prison is the microcosm of society, the exemplary institution because there individuals are openly known in order to be controlled, so that they may be utilized and commodified in the most productive manner possible. The "carceral continuum," as Foucault calls it, seems to be the logical finale of the socioeconomic enterprise of capitalism. Those of us generally characterized as humanist intellectuals often like to think we stand outside. Unlike technointellectuals—the sons of Frederick Taylor who manage our factories, universities, hospitals, and prisons—we, at any rate, do not work as engineers of the carceral system. Or so we must think. But

Foucault will not exempt us: educators at all levels are for him prime examples of the channeling and application of knowledge/power.[10]

With his concept of intellection as rhetoricopolitical activity, Burke joins Foucault. Burke's intellectual "identifies" his audience in order to "transform" it. We want again to ask, to what end? But I do not think that we should ask that question in *a priori* fashion, as if "the intellectual" really represented an autonomous class, crystallized and separated out from socioeconomic matrices. To ask the question of the intellectual in that way is already to accept what Gramsci called the "traditional intellectual" on his own terms; it is to accept uncritically his idealistic vocation as a student of ideas and a keeper of culture, as if such vocation had never been severely tested by Marx and Engels in *The German Ideology.* The question will have to be rooted in what Foucault calls the "specific intellectual," working from a particular social and historical experience, within a specific place in the institutional network: the question must be so framed even though the intellectual (the academic intellectual in particular) will tend to regard himself as a cosmopolitan, universal figure, dispassionately attached *as intellectual* to the society in which he lives, speaking for the ages, and even though he will tend to think that when he serves culture he stands outside power—which is not the case, he will readily admit, when he pays taxes, votes, or buys groceries.

To come to cases: though we cannot ask the question Platonically, we can ask it specifically here of Kenneth Burke. We can ask whether Burke himself conceives of himself as an autonomous thinker; whether so self-deceived he permits himself to be appropriated for the better reinforcement of the disciplined society. Though there is no univocal answer to the question, I believe that Burke functioned for the most part as a critical intellectual whose rhetorical activity of identification and would-be transformation moves toward an emancipating ideal of sociopolitical self-awareness. Burke is mainly convinced that traditional American liberal ideals cannot make us free—that the liberal norm of autonomy in particular, as it defines us in our occupational identity and especially, I would add, as it defines teachers in traditional academic settings, is not only deceptive for the intellectual: it permits him to deceive the sheep as well. Thus do humanists help to fashion the hegemony that will keep us, and themselves, in the dark.

Burke's conception of himself as critical rhetor demands that he lay bare the hegemonic process in all its subtle and insidious ways. He says: "We are clearly in the region of rhetoric when considering the identification whereby a specialized activity makes one a participant in some social or economic class. 'Belonging' in this sense is rhetorical."[11] As he works this region of rhetoric, he is concerned not only to bring to the consciousness of his audience their identification as individuals with a "class" or, if that word is too Old World for Americans, then we must say their involvement, socially and economically, with an "interest" group. In the land of the new Adam and Eve, the isolato, as Melville called the American self—a darker measuring of that most happy fellow, the rugged individual—such consciousness is rarer than we think. Burke's purpose in identifying such consciousness and revealing to it its identifications is not to form social self-consciousness for its own sake or, in the current mode, to encourage a micro-politics. His goals are neither contemplative nor Foucauldian. The widening of consciousness is a necessary first step to a different kind of praxis, one that is not content merely to work its "autonomous" activity and then give up, refuse to take its work home, declaring its impotence with "that is not my field," and other statements which absolve us from the uses to which our work is put. Burke wants us to take our work home. His effort to undermine our feeling of autonomy, to make us feel responsible to the larger social project, to the social whole, is an effort to bring to birth, out of our fragmented existences, an organic identity that would be rooted in a critical power to coordinate and integrate the separate levels of our lives: to make us whole again beyond confusion. That is a redemptive project, one which would put us back in control, and shatter the image of Orwellian progress narrated in *Discipline and Punish*. Everything is "our business":

> If the technical expert, as such, is assigned the task of perfecting new powers of chemical, bacteriological, or atomic destruction, his morality *as technical expert* requires only that he apply himself to his task as effectively as possible. The question of what the new force might mean, as released into a social texture emotionally and intellectually unfit to control it, or as

surrendered to men whose *specialty* is *professional killing*—well, that is simply "none of our business," as specialists, however great may be his misgivings as father of a family, or as citizen of his nation and of the world.[12]

It is always easy for humanists, too easy, to score ethical points off the myopic among technocrats and scientists. Burke won't indulge such self-righteousness; he won't let us off the hook. *A Rhetoric of Motives*, published in 1950, was mostly written in the late 1940s. In the passage I've just quoted on nuclear scientists and professional killers, we should feel the pressure of the Manhattan Project, the Cold War, and the anguish of Robert Oppenheimer. In the passage I am about to quote, Burke reflects on the literary-critical wars of the thirties and forties. Specialists in literary technology come off ethically not much better than specialists in atomic destruction: "So much progressive and radical criticism in recent years has been concerned with the social implications of art, that affirmations of art's autonomy can often become, by antithesis, a roundabout way of identifying oneself with the interests of political conservatism. In accordance with the rhetorical principle of identification, whenever you find a doctrine of 'nonpolitical' esthetics affirmed with fervor, look for its politics."[13]

2

In the title essay of *The Philosophy of Literary Form* Burke defines "symbolic action" by offering in its place a series of metonymic substitutions whose cumulative effect is to broaden immensely the scope of the term "literary" in his title. His key substitutions are "strategy," "magical decree," "scapegoat," "fetish," "name," and, father of them all, "representation." For Burke these nouns always need to be converted to their active verbal form—"decreeing," "scapegoating," "fetishizing," and so on, all of which are best understood by a term that must qualify as one of his favorites: "encompassment," writing as a technique of "encompassing," an attempt to master a situation, a will to power.

Considered in such light, his traditional term for symbolic action, "representation," carries none of the freight that it is generally made to carry in the history of mimetic theories of art. Symbolic action as "representation" is an activity simply charged with power, an activity we can call aesthetic praxis provided that we understand the aesthetic against the grain of the highly specialized meaning that tends to dominate thought about literature and art since the late eighteenth century. Against the grain we retrieve a more classical sense of the aesthetic *as* the practical and *as* the rhetorical: the aesthetic as the sine qua non of the cultural economy.[14]

Burke says, "I feel it to be no mere accident of language that we use the same word for sensory, artistic, and political representation."[15] The inherent claim of any sort of representation, the basis, as the case may be, of its epistemological, or aesthetic, or sociopolitical authority (Burke would blur those categories), the basis of its coercive power is an ontological claim, used like a hammer, that some part of the whole *really does* stand in for the whole—participates in the whole. At the level of concept, we need a neo-Platonic sense of "participation" to grasp Burke's point; at the rhetorical level, either openly or (more frequently) covertly, representation appears under the figure of synecdoche, Burke's master trope for the part/whole relationship. The discourse of synecdoche asserts itself as a relationship of signifier and signified that is not arbitrary. To assent to the "truth" of a representation/synecdoche, then, is to assent to its profoundest claim: that of epistemological and ontological universality. And it is to assent necessarily and concomitantly to a profoundly repressive discourse. In the name of universality and truth, representation becomes a cover-up in two ways: it hides itself as an agency of specific political power, as a highly specified and structured social text, and in the same process it covers up social and cultural difference and conflict within the social text. Writing, as Derrida has argued, is unthinkable without repression—I choose to understand him to be making a statement about the inherent politics of writing.[16]

The theoretical text in the Western tradition most responsible for this complex sense of representation (though not consciously) is the *Poetics* of Aristotle—where we learn most of what we need to know about the deviousness of mimesis if we confront Aristotle with himself: if we place alongside the ninth chapter of the *Poetics*, in which the universality of "poetry" is argued at the expense of "history"—even as both are subordinated to philosophy: an unblemished mirror of the truth of universals—his fifteenth chapter (and related parts of the *Politics*) in which the proper representation of character, its "necessary" and "probable" mimesis according to the dictates of human nature, is stipulated by bringing forth the examples of women and slaves, one of which is said by nature to be inferior and the other, by the same eternal standard, is declared worthless. (All character typologies in the classical tradition should be read in the context of this source.) Aristotle is saying that if you would represent women and slaves in a fashion that would satisfy the conditions of human nature, if you want to persuade reason's tribunal, philosophy itself, then you must not give them the qualities appropriate only to a free male. Though it is his intention to tell us otherwise, at a certain level the text of the *Poetics*, because it is bound over to the larger cultural intentionality of his society, works against his ontological claim for the universal (and his claim for reason as ahistorical arbiter) and shows that representations are always culturally and politically specific, and in doing this the *Poetics* reveals, to our chagrin, that the material basis of its continuing cultural power resides in a slave-holding society. Yet as a "traditional" text, to come back to that difficult concept (which is how we have received it and how, according to the dominant paradigm of reading, we should understand it), its material basis is hidden by the eliding action of our tradition-making, beginning most forcefully in the Italian Renaissance, so that its universalist claims for mimesis are freed from the socially specific moment within which they were made. Against the traditional reading, I am making this claim: the *Poetics* says that "poetry" is better than "history" because it makes "reasonable" the specific "equipment for living" deployed by ruling-class Greek men in classical Athens.

One of Burke's strengths is that he understood the treachery of the traditionalist intellect early, and he knew it overtly. With ironic understatement of the issues involved he writes: "In theories of politics prevailing at different periods in history, there have been quarrels as to the precise vessel of authority that is to be considered 'representative' of the society as a whole . . . but all agree in assuming that there is *some* part representative of the whole, hence fit to stand for it."[17] The "agreement" that such is the case is the mask of a desire that it be so. Political and by implication aesthetic representations are revealed in their intentional force, as productions of a collective will to power when, in periods of social crisis, "an authoritative class, whose purpose and ideals had been generally considered as *representative* of the total society's purposes and ideals, becomes considered as *antagonistic*. Their class character, once felt to be a *culminating* part of the whole, is now felt to be a *divisive* part of the whole."[18] Under the pressure of Burke's analysis the term "representation" becomes a sign of the convergence of the political and the aesthetic, and of the complicity of the aesthetic with political power. The aesthetic is always traversed by power; never does it stand "outside" in a universal situated beyond the work of will. Again, however, and this cannot, I believe, be said too forcefully, the convergence of the political and the aesthetic is not necessarily a convergence of the aesthetic with the politically progressive (which, in different ways, is a sentimental argument sometimes made by both Lukács and Marcuse). We shouldn't forget the significance of the fifteenth chapter of the *Poetics* or, more dramatically, Burke's work on Hitler's artistry.

Hitler was a kind of medicine man, but then, as Burke reminds us, so are all poets.[19] The poet as medicine man, as political doctor: the diseases he would attend to infest the body politic; his medicine is a representation charged with power's purposiveness. To define representation in this way is to define it as rhetoric, and according to Burke aesthetic-rhetorical medicine has but two uses—it can be therapeutic or prophylactic. The common denominator in either function is that the aesthetic becomes a part of the *consolatio philosophiae*: "It would protect us. Let us remind ourselves, however, that implicit in the idea of protection there is the idea of something to be *protected against*. Hence, to analyze the element of *comfort* in beauty, without false emphasis, we must be less monistic, more 'dialectical,' in that we include also, as an important aspect of the recipe, the element of *discomfort* (actual or threatened) for which the poetry is 'medicine.' "[20] Burke explains that this dialectical sense of the aesthetic is to be retrieved from older theories of art that stress affect rather than interpretation. In ancient and Renaissance traditions, art exists as a type of cultural power, for the purpose of educating and moving, not for the purpose of interpretation. Beauty then should be taken in the context of the sublime (as a type of action) rather than in a nineteenth-century context of formalistic autonomy (as pure contemplation). In his proposal to replace our sense of beauty as "pure" representation by reading the beautiful through the impure category of the sublime (some "vastness of magnitude, power, or distance, disproportionate to ourselves"), Burke tells us that beauty's basis cannot be located monistically in an "in itself"—in some inert and isolated object or in a self conceived in its essential subjectiveness as prior to, or at least outside what we call society: "Confronting the poetic act in terms of the sublime and the ridiculous, we are disposed to think of the issue in terms *of a situation and a strategy for confronting or encompassing that situation*, a scene and an act, with each possessing its own genius, but the two fields interwoven."[21] For Burke, the beautiful understood as the sublime is an image of social struggle. With a threat as its basis, beauty cannot be conceived monistically but only dialectically as always an act in the world, always involved in the administration of political medicine. Burke's Longinus, unlike Curtius's, is a theorist of aesthetic power.

Burke encapsulates his theory of poetic expression and in the process darkens his medical metaphor by appealing to the story of Perseus and the Medusa, a myth more central to poetics, from his point of view, than the story of Orpheus and his voyage to Hades: "Perseus who could not face the serpent-headed monster without being turned to stone, but was immune to this danger if he observed it to be a reflection in a mirror."[22] The mirror of Perseus does what Burke insists representation cannot help doing—it represents with a difference; it bears purpose; it is itself an act of power in that it controls the murderous Medusa and, performing this initial act, prepares for another: the decapitation of the Medusa. Burke would have us read the myth of Perseus as a tale of the political work of the aesthetic. It is a tale that tells us what he has told us in other, perhaps less striking ways—that literature makes something happen, that the literary is always the taking of position and simultaneously the exercising of position within and upon the social field. Thus: Hitler's rhetoric functioned as a representation of the German people, Jews and non-Jews alike; his representation bore a certain powerful purpose: it controlled the German people. By performing this initial act of power, it prepared for another—an act of genocide. And that act, whether viewed in its horrifying physical dimension, or in its not unhorrifying rhetorical dimension (these two cannot finally be separated) and all the preparatory acts that led up to it—including a certain reading of Nietzsche, as Derrida has suggested—let us not soften the point: this act of genocide and the acts which necessarily preceded it functioned, and continue to function, in the manner of the *consolatio philosophiae*: they functioned, and continue to function, for a certain audience, as therapy.

It is likely, I think, that many of us trained in literature, because of what that training did to us and pretty much continues to do to our students, it is likely that Burke's essay on Hitler will cause many of us so formed to make certain statements: "But *Mein Kampf* is not literature." Or: "*Mein Kampf* may be literature, but it is bad literature." The Burkean answer to these head-in-the-sand responses must be: "Not only is *Mein Kampf* literature; it was highly effective literature." If we need to believe otherwise, and literary people too often need to believe otherwise (I speak not from the outside on this matter); if we need to believe that literature is somehow always involved in a noble, humane cause, a position common on the literary left as well as the literary right and center (what else can be on our minds when we urge that our undergraduates read the classics of the Western tradition?), then let us at least be shaken by Burke's subversion of the sentiment that literature is inherently humane. Literature is inherently nothing; or it is inherently a body of rhetorical strategies waiting to be seized. And anybody can seize them. Literature is not Keats. The literary is never only the elite canon of great books; it is also what we call "minor" literature and "popular" literature. But it is more even than what this expanded definition would allow. It is all writing considered as social practice, all writing viewed in its material circumstances and in its purposiveness. It is power as representation. The literary is all around us, and it is always doing its work upon us. It bears the past in many complex ways, but it does its deed, makes its mark, marks us, here and now. The knowledge that the literary is present power (in Burke's sense of "present") cannot, of course, free us from power, though that knowledge is somewhat salutary especially because modern literary theory has not much wanted to know about power. We need to know that what is therapeutic or prophylactic for some is poison for others; that the literary cannot free itself from this double effect; that it is always efficacious, one way or another; that as writers and teachers we dispense drugs every day.

Of course no one wants to dispense poison to one's readers and students; one wants to be the good doctor. And in fact it is very difficult to define a role for the intellectual not grounded on that feeling—though Foucault has tried. It is probably not a simple matter of choosing not to dispense poison—were it so, the intellectual life would be a good deal simpler, and all honor would be ours. I'll put this personally: I have been tempted to offer Burke as the angel of modern criticism, an unambiguous good in the midst of all this bad. In more than one place in the preceding pages I have tried to resist this urge, but let me here bring this problem down to one case. My reader will have noticed the repeated occurrence of the figure of Babel in Burke's work— an image, variously, of linguistic divisiveness and chaos, hermeneutic solipsism, social struggle, the scene of rhetoric, the condition of exile from a unified, paradisal community, or even, for the antinomian soul, the Burkean soul, paradise itself. The figure occurs early and late in Burke's work. For reasons which I've explored, and won't bother to rehearse, he has considered the idea, sometimes with horror, other times with pleasure. What I have not yet mentioned, however, is that the figure of Babel occurs centrally in his essay on Hitler, whom Burke finds offering the German people, as an alternative to the many-voiced confusion of their parliament (a "vocal diaspora"), his single, mastering voice and presence, a unifying center interchangeable with Munich. The figure of Babel is an awful point of convergence: Hitler not as exterior bad from which we can protect ourselves by the proper cherishing of his negation, whoever or whatever that might be, but as figure himself of an ultimate impulse to essentialization inside any and all of our good angels. What has Burke found in Hitler if not a fun-house mirror reflection of tendencies within his own theories of interpretation? Assuming that Burke was well aware of the repeated figuration of Babel in his own writings, it is something of an astonishment that he undertook the essay on *Mein Kampf* at all. Having once undertaken it, it is to his credit that he did not bury the "familiar" figure he encountered in Hitler's book. Perhaps, then, there is yet another and finer quality of critical consciousness that this episode reveals: that finer quality, through its clarity, its accessibility, its refusal to revise its past, its refusal to pose as all-knowing, is nothing other than a quality that permits itself, the critical consciousness itself, *to be criticized*—the teacher become student, the critic become text, the doctor become patient. And perhaps that is the best one can give to one's students and readers: the means to resist oneself. Especially a criticism that would work for the alleviation of repression cannot afford to do less. It must make itself vulnerable; failure to do so will bring against its efforts the reactions of contempt which history always keeps waiting in the wings in readiness to expose false humanists.[23]

3

What is the rhetoric of *A Rhetoric of Motives*? Burke spoke of two purposes for writing the book: first, to bring rhetoric back into the literary against the effort of theoreticians of the aesthetic to banish rhetoric from the realm of the literary; second, to revise the traditional idea of rhetoric so that, newly conceived, it could stand between pure deliberate activity and the unconscious: "There is an intermediate area of expression that is not wholly deliberate, yet not wholly unconscious. It lies midway between aimless utterance and speech directly purposive."[24] "Speech directly purposive" stands, of course, as a definition of rhetoric in its classical, overtly political project, while "aimless utterance" signifies what the literary has become from Kant to de Man: discourse presumably apolitical, unrhetorical, without a design, as in the Kantian formula "purposiveness without purpose," or discourse, as in de Man's mode, whose designs incessantly subvert themselves—self-deconstructive writing, politics necessarily unfulfilled, frustrated rhetoric constantly turning against itself. Burkean rhetoric would occupy the space between the old rheto-

ric of pure will and the modernist and postmodernist aesthetic of
antiwill: between a subject apparently in full possession of itself,
and in full intentional control of its expression, and a subject
whose relation to "its" expression is very problematic. (My use of
the possessive "its" can be traced ultimately to a convention of
thinking about expression and its source put to shame by philosophers as diverse as Kant, Nietzsche, Derrida, and Foucault.)
Burke is giving rhetoric an unconscious, something unheard of in
the ancient traditions, but in the process of doing so he is not
going to lose sight of the conscious and the willful.

In the little fable of history as conversation that I am about to
quote the conversants are simultaneously the innocent targets of
history and its responsible executors, both subjected to the coercive power of the past and the accountable makers of the future.
Similarly in Burke's theory of rhetoric: the rhetorician is the
not-always-knowing carrier of historical and ideological forces,
while at the same time he acts within and upon the present and
thereby becomes an agent of change. Burke's metaphor of conversation, unlike Richard Rorty's, is from the beginning a
metaphor of social text, of how that text makes us and of how we
make *it*, both for ourselves and for the future. The primal scene of
rhetoric is the unending conversation of history:

> Imagine that you enter a parlor. You come late. When you
> arrive, others have long preceded you, and they are engaged
> in a heated discussion, a discussion too heated for them to
> pause and tell you exactly what it is about. In fact, the discus-
> sion had already begun long before any of them got there, so
> that no one present is qualified to retrace for you all the steps
> that had gone before. You listen for a while, until you decide
> that you have caught the tenor of the argument; then you put
> in your oar. Someone answers; you answer him; another
> comes to your defense; another aligns himself against you, to
> either the embarrassment or gratification of your opponent,
> depending upon the quality of your ally's assistance. How-
> ever, the discussion is interminable. The hour grows late, you
> must depart. And you do depart, with the discussion still
> vigorously in progress.[25]

Burke's domestic setting of rhetoric's historical scene is itself
rhetorically shrewd. We are at home. Without flourish he sac-
rifices the usual Olympian grandeur that goes with such subjects

in order to tell us that rhetoric and history are mostly just where we are, most of the time.

We enter a parlor and we are late—not by accident but by necessity. Others are already there, and they are so involved that they can't stop to fill us in. So we can't know what we would ideally like to know about the scene we've entered, but neither does anyone else, because no one was there, at the beginning, when the conversation started. No one is therefore qualified to "retrace" for us all the steps that have gone before. In fact, no one has ever been so qualified; strictly speaking, we aren't even allowed to say that the conversation "started." As in a dream, we find ourselves there: simply *there*. And we are late because, in dreams and in history, that is the way things are. We feel a pressure from the past exerting itself powerfully upon us through the conversation now taking place; whatever it is, nightmare or history, we are definitely in it. We didn't ask to be in it; we don't know what we think we need to know; and we can never know it. People make conversations, but this one is bigger than anybody. We feel burdened immensely; we are not the master.

Then we act; we just do. We *decide*, with what assurances Burke never says, because there are none to be given. We enter the conversation by putting in our "oar" (our "or"?). It matters not that no one in the room really knows, in the strict epistemological sense of "knowing," what is going on; or that no one who has ever been in the room ever knew. This is a conversation without epistemological "foundation" or "substance." The fact is that we are going to argue with one another, heatedly, and the argument is not going to come to a conclusion, ever, because more people, in similar states of historically burdened ignorance, are going to come into the room. The only thing that can come to conclusion is ourselves: "You must depart. And you do depart, with the discussion still vigorously in progress." Burke's fable for history has a double moral. History is a masterful, powerful process: it "makes" us, and yet, at the same time, at any moment in the process, our active willing "makes" the conversation, gives it the propulsive energy that forces it on. So even though we may feel "mastered," by putting in our oars we do two things: we help to shape our own experience of history *while providing the shape of things to come for those who will enter later*, after we are gone.

Burke's fable is dialectical through and through. The scene of history and the scene of rhetoric are inseparable (in-"term"-inable).

Situated in a scene of history and willing that complicated, the rhetorical act as Burke understands it will imply other conditions no less fundamental, perhaps corollaries of its basic condition. Rhetoric's first condition constitutes something like an existential argument for freedom. Though he calls this a traditional principle of rhetoric, his point about freedom is compatible with Nietzsche's disposition, yet I do not see the new Nietzscheans paying any attention to it. In Burke's words: "Persuasion involves choice, will; it is directed to man only insofar as he is *free*. This is good to remember, in these days of dictatorship and near-dictatorship. Only insofar as men are potentially free, must the spellbinder seek to persuade them. Insofar as they *must* do something, rhetoric is unnecessary, its work being done by the nature of things, though often these necessities are not of a natural origin, but come from necessities imposed by man-made conditions . . . that sometimes [flow] from the nature of the 'free market.' "[26]

Determinism will permit no rhetoric. With its assumption of freedom, implicitly expressed in its every attempt to change the minds of others, rhetoric becomes the enemy, at least potentially, even of those perverse determinist schemes of thought and social organization that would employ rhetoric to defeat all willing. In Burke's provocative example, rhetoric itself subverts the naturalization of society, under the name of capitalism, that would submit us to the laws of political economy. Like Burke's antinomian aesthetic, rhetoric, rigorously pursued, will undermine any rigid and repressive scheme of living. Rhetoric is not the figural undoing of all action, as de Man claims in the name of Nietzsche: it is the very soul of action, potentially the good angel of change that could prevail against all determinist perversions of rhetoric. I do not say "it will," or "it must," because it is of the implicit nature of rhetoric to deny "it must" (even when it uses "it must" to accomplish its goals).

The second of rhetoric's conditions, Burke calls it "the characteristic invitation to rhetoric," involves a fundamental concern of social theory. Let us call it the potential for community. What characteristically invites rhetoric's activity is a social situation somewhere between pure identification of interests and absolute separation. In pure identification, while many kinds of human difference would remain, all differences of ideology would be resolved in a utopian commonality that would put us beyond the struggles that destroy the spirit. In utopian ideological identity there would be no need for rhetoric. "Likewise, there would be no strife in absolute separateness, since opponents can join battle only through a mediating ground that makes their communication possible, thus providing the first condition necessary for the exchange of blows." In absolute separateness there is no possibility for rhetoric. "But put identification and division ambiguously together, so that you cannot know for certain just where one ends and the other begins, and you have the characteristic invitation to rhetoric." In a world of agonistic stress, rhetoric would move inexorably toward the dream of perfect social organization, the achievement of which would cause rhetoric to self-destruct in the euphoria of real communion.[27]

But whose dream of community? Community founded, to cite Foucault's terms, upon a vertical, or a horizontal principle of human relations? Since the strategies of rhetoric are radically appropriable, since rhetoric as such favors no particular vision of community and the good life, those questions can have no *a priori* answers. Perfect community will require the elimination of the agon, but the word "elimination" is horribly ambiguous. Do we mean the "reconciliation" of agonistic elements through the healing power of a truly embracing human vision? Or do we mean "elimination" as exclusion, negation, exile, and murder? Since the dangerous game of rhetoric is open to all, since we are all always already involved: since, to come to an issue important to me, the historical fate and status of Marxism will not be decided by the irreversible narrative force of history (the appeal to teleology can only be a rhetorical ploy, a strategy perhaps worthy in times like ours, in the United States, when everything seems to be flowing the wrong way, when, therefore, we require patience and spiritual bracing—the appeal is not a reference to a promised end that must be), then the fate of Marxism will be decided by the active involvement of individuals in the great struggle of persuasion. To say this about the fate of socialism, that it will be decided in rhetorical war, is to say nothing especially specific to its vision. The fate of all visions, or nightmares, as the case may be, of the good life, will be similarly decided.

"Decided" is too weak: "chosen."

Notes

Provocations

1. Kenneth Burke, *Attitudes Toward History* (Boston: Beacon Press, 1961), pp. 331–32.

2. Michel Foucault, *Discipline and Punish: The Birth of the Prison*, trans. Alan Sheridan (New York: Pantheon Books, 1977), p. 136. Also see my two-part essay in the 1982 Spring and Summer issues of *Raritan*: "Reading Foucault (Punishment, Labor, Resistance)."

3. *Attitudes Toward History*, p. 332.

4. The quotation is from William James, *The Principles of Psychology*, (New York: Dover Publications, Inc., 1950), 1:8. The conclusions that I draw from it are partly my own and partly John Dewey's in *Philosophy and Civilization* (New York: Capricorn Books, 1963), pp. 13–35.

5. *The Philosophy of John Dewey*, ed. with an introduction and commentary by John J. McDermott (Chicago: University of Chicago Press, 1981), p. 370.

6. See F. O. Matthiessen, *The James Family* (New York: Alfred A. Knopf, 1961), p. 633, for James's statement on behalf of the individual and against collectivity.

7. On connecting phenomenology and totalitarianism, see Herbert Marcuse, *Negations: Essays in Critical Theory*, trans. Jeremy J. Shapiro (Boston: Beacon Press, 1968), pp. 63–64.

8. Michel Foucault, *Power/Knowledge: Selected Interviews and Other Writings, 1972–1977*, ed. Colin Gordon, trans. Colin Gordon, Leo Marshall, John Mepham, and Kate Soper (New York: Pantheon Books, 1980), pp. 126–33.

9. Edward W. Said, "Opponents, Audiences, Constituencies, and Community," *Critical Inquiry* 9 (September 1982): 15.

10. Karl Marx and Frederick Engels, *The German Ideology*, ed., with an introduction by C. J. Arthur (New York: International Publishers, 1970), p. 123—the eleventh thesis on Feuerbach.

11. *The Selected Writings of Ralph Waldo Emerson*, ed. with a biographical introduction by Brooks Atkinson, foreword by Tremaine McDowell (New York: Modern Library, 1968), pp. 149–50.

12. *Attitudes Toward History*, pp. 332–33.

13. Quoted in Raymond Williams, *Keywords: A Vocabulary of Culture and Society* (New York: Oxford University Press, 1976), pp. 76–82.

14. Edward W. Said, *The World, the Text, and the Critic* (Cambridge, Mass.: Harvard University Press, 1983), pp. 8–12.

15. Raymond Williams, *Marxism and Literature* (New York: Oxford University Press, 1977), pp. 112–13.

16. Richard Rorty, *Philosophy and the Mirror of Nature* (Princeton, N.J.: Princeton University Press, 1979), p. 379. The source in Dewey is *The Public and Its Problems*; see the excerpt in *The Philosophy of John Dewey*, p. 642.

17. *Philosophy and the Mirror of Nature*, p. 378 and "Part Three" throughout for the position that produces this kind of statement.

18. Ibid., p. 360. "For edifying discourse is supposed to be abnormal, to take us out of ourselves by the power of strangeness, to aid us in becoming new beings." Romantics from Coleridge to Hulme, Ransom, and the Russian Formalists would agree.

19. Richard Rorty, *Consequences of Pragmatism (Essays: 1972–1980)* (Minneapolis: University of Minnesota Press, 1982), pp. 191–210.

20. Ibid., esp. pp. 203–8.

21. Ibid., p. 210.

22. Ibid., pp. 203, 207.

23. John Dewey: "The attainment of a state of society in which a basis of material security will release the powers of individuals for cultural expression is not the work of a day" (from *Liberalism and Social Action*, as excerpted in *The Philosophy of John Dewey*).

Part One

1. Quoted in Ben Yagoda, "Kenneth Burke," *Horizon* 23 (June 1980): 68.

2. Ibid.

3. Ibid.

4. Kenneth Burke, "Revolutionary Symbolism in America," *American Writers' Congress*, ed. Henry Hart (New York: International Publishers, 1935), p. 87.

5. Karl Marx and Frederick Engels, *The German Ideology*, ed. with an introduction by C. J. Arthur (New York: International Publishers, 1970), p. 121.

6. "Revolutionary Symbolism in America," p. 87.

7. Ibid., p. 88.

8. Ibid.

9. Ibid., pp. 88–89.

10. For the quotation from Burke, see p. 89. For Marx and Engels on "representation," see *The German Ideology*, pp. 65–66.

11. "Revolutionary Symbolism in America," p. 89.

12. Ibid.

13. Ibid.

14. Ibid.

15. Ibid.

16. Ibid., pp. 89–90.

17. Ibid., p. 90.

18. Ibid., p. 91.

19. Ibid.

20. Ibid.

21. Ibid.

22. Ibid., p. 92.

23. Ibid., p. 93.

24. Ibid.

25. Ibid.

26. Paul de Man, *Allegories of Reading: Figural Language in Rousseau, Nietzsche, Rilke, and Proust* (New Haven, Conn.: Yale University Press, 1979), pp. 16–17.

27. Paul de Man, *Mallarmé, Yeats, and the Post-Romantic Predicament* (Harvard University Diss., May 1960), pp. 54, 84.

28. Ibid., p. 102n.

29. *Allegories of Reading*, p. 131.

30. Paul de Man, *Blindness and Insight: Essays in the Rhetoric of Contemporary Criticism* (New York: Oxford University Press, 1971), p. 165.

31. Ibid., p. 142.

32. Ibid., p. 144.

33. Ibid., p. 146.

34. Ibid., p. 147.

35. Ibid., p. 150.

36. Ibid., pp. 148, 150.

37. Ibid., p. 151.

38. Ibid.

39. Ibid., pp. 151–52.

40. Ibid., p. 151.

41. Ibid., p. 152.

42. Ibid., p. 154.

43. Ibid., pp. 156–57.

44. Ibid., p. 157.

45. Ibid., p. 159.

46. Ibid., p. 163.

47. *Selections from the Prison Notebooks of Antonio Gramsci*, ed. and

trans. Quintin Hoare and Geoffrey Nowell Smith (New York: International Publishers, 1971), p. 360.

48. *Blindness and Insight*, p. 161.
49. Ibid.
50. Ibid., p. 162.
51. Ibid.
52. Ibid., p. 165.

Part Two

1. Raymond Williams, *Keywords: A Vocabulary of Culture and Society* (New York: Oxford University Press, 1976), pp. 150–54.

2. Kenneth Burke, *The Philosophy of Literary Form: Studies in Symbolic Action* (Berkeley and Los Angeles: University of California Press, 1973), p. 23.

3. See Jacques Derrida, *Positions*, trans. and annotated by Alan Bass (Chicago: University of Chicago Press, 1981), pp. 56–58, for a penetrating discussion of this point.

4. Kenneth Burke, *Permanence and Change: An Anatomy of Purpose* (Los Altos, Calif.: Hermes Publications, 1954), p. 5.

5. Ibid., pp. 5–6.
6. Ibid., p. 35.
7. Ibid., pp. 117–18.
8. Ibid., p. 226.
9. Ibid., p. 228.
10. *The Philosophy of Literary Form*, pp. 261–62.

11. Kenneth Burke, *Attitudes Toward History* (Boston: Beacon Press, 1961), p. vii.

12. Ibid., p. 225.
13. Ibid., pp. 225–26.
14. Ibid., p. 171.

15. W. K. Wimsatt and Cleanth Brooks, *Literary Criticism: A Short History* (New York: Alfred A. Knopf, 1962), p. vii.

16. Paul de Man, "Political Allegory in Rousseau," *Critical Inquiry* 2 (Summer 1976): 650.

17. *Attitudes Toward History*, pp. 41–42.
18. Ibid., p. 43.
19. *The Philosophy of Literary Form*, p. 34.
20. Ibid., p. 105.
21. Ibid., p. 106.
22. Ibid., pp. 109–11n.

23. Kenneth Burke, *A Grammar of Motives* (Berkeley and Los Angeles: University of California Press, 1969), p. xv.

24. Ibid.
25. Ibid.
26. Ibid., p. xvi.
27. Ibid.
28. Ibid., pp. xxii–xxiii.
29. *The Philosophy of Literary Form*, p. 109n.
30. *A Grammar of Motives*, p. xviii.
31. Ibid., p. xix.
32. Ibid., p. 128.
33. Ibid., p. 66.
34. Ibid., pp. 68–69.
35. Ibid., p. 40.
36. Ibid., p. 23.
37. Ibid.
38. Ibid., p. 24.
39. Ibid.
40. See, for example, *Selections from the Prison Notebooks*, ed. and trans. Quintin Hoare and Geoffrey Nowell Smith (New York: International Publishers, 1971), pp. 5–14. For important commentary, see Walter L. Adamson, *Hegemony and Revolution: A Study of Antonio Gramsci's Political and Cultural Theory* (Berkeley and Los Angeles: University of California Press, 1980).
41. *Attitudes Toward History*, p. 329.
42. *The Philosophy of Literary Form*, p. 307.
43. *Attitudes Toward History*, pp. 329–30.
44. *The Philosophy of Literary Form*, p. 305.
45. *Attitudes Toward History*, p. 216.
46. *The Philosophy of Literary Form*, pp. 41–42.
47. *Attitudes Toward History*, pp. 124–34.
48. Ibid., p. 94.
49. Nicos Poulantzas, *Political Power and Social Classes*, trans. Timothy O'Hagan (London: New Left Books, 1973), pp. 13–16.
50. *Attitudes Toward History*, p. 135. See also Fredric Jameson, *The Political Unconscious: Narrative as a Socially Symbolic Act* (Ithaca, N.Y.: Cornell University Press, 1981), p. 95.
51. *Attitudes Toward History*, p. 328.
52. Michel Foucault, *Language, Counter-Memory, Practice*, ed. with an introduction by Donald F. Bouchard, trans. Donald F. Bouchard and Sherry Simon (Ithaca, N.Y.: Cornell University Press, 1977), p. 154.
53. *Attitudes Toward History*, p. 328.
54. *The Philosophy of Literary Form*, pp. 109–11n.
55. *Attitudes Toward History*, p. 66n.
56. Ibid., p. 129.

57. Ibid., p. 128.
58. Ibid., p. 129.
59. Ibid., p. 66n.
60. *A Grammar of Motives*, p. 153.
61. Quoted in Ibid., p. 154.
62. Ibid., p. 156.
63. Ibid., p. 158.

Part Three

1. Quoted in Ben Yagoda, "Kenneth Burke," *Horizon* 23 (June 1980): 67.
2. Kenneth Burke, *A Rhetoric of Motives* (Berkeley and Los Angeles: University of California Press, 1969), p. 27.
3. Ibid., pp. 30–31.
4. Kenneth Burke, *Counter-Statement* (Berkeley and Los Angeles: University of California Press, 1968), p. viii.
5. Ibid., p. ix.
6. Ibid., p. 31.
7. Ibid., p. 123.
8. Ibid., pp. 37–42, 35, 41, 46.
9. Ibid., p. 48.
10. W. B. Yeats, "The Autumn of the Body," in *Essays and Introductions* (New York: Macmillan Publishing Co., 1961), pp. 189–92.
11. Karl Marx, *Capital*, introduction by Ernest Mandel, trans. Ben Fowkes (New York: Vintage Books, 1977), 1:131.
12. *Counter-Statement*, p. 63.
13. Georg Lukács, *History and Class Consciousness*, trans. Rodney Livingstone (Cambridge, Mass.: MIT Press, 1971). See the discussions of Kant in "Reification and the Consciousness of the Proletariat."
14. Karl Marx, *Capital*, ed. Frederick Engels, trans. Samuel Moore and Edward Aveling (New York: International Publishers, 1967), 3:820.
15. *Counter-Statement*, p. 64.
16. Ibid., p. 65.
17. Ibid., p. 66.
18. Ibid., p. 67.
19. Ibid., p. 68.
20. Ibid., p. 69.
21. Ibid., p. 80.
22. Ibid.
23. Ibid., p. 290.
24. Ibid., p. 163.
25. Ibid., pp. 146–47.

26. Ibid., p. 147.
27. *A Rhetoric of Motives*, p. 41; *Counter-Statement*, p. 163.
28. *Counter-Statement*, p. 111.
29. Ibid.
30. Ibid., p. 112.
31. Ibid., p. 114.
32. Edmund Wilson, *Axel's Castle: A Study in the Imaginative Literature of 1870–1930* (New York: Charles Scribner's Sons, 1931), pp. 279, 282, 283.
33. Ibid., pp. 298, 276, 293.
34. *Counter-Statement*, p. 71.

Part Four

1. Friedrich Nietzsche, *The Use and Abuse of History*, trans. Adrian Collins, with an introduction by Julius Kraft (Indianapolis, Ind.: Bobbs-Merrill Co. Inc., 1977), p. 6.
2. Kenneth Burke, *Counter-Statement* (Berkeley and Los Angeles: University of California Press, 1968), p. 108.
3. Ibid.
4. Jacques Derrida, "Differance," in *Speech and Phenomena, and Other Essays on Husserl's Theory of Signs*, trans. with an introduction by David B. Allison, preface by Newton Garver (Evanston, Ill.: Northwestern University Press, 1973), pp. 142–43.
5. *Counter-Statement*, p. 110.
6. Kenneth Burke, *Attitudes Toward History* (Boston: Beacon Press, 1961), p. 201.
7. Louis Althusser, *Reading Capital*, trans. Ben Brewster (London: New Left Books, 1970), p. 94.
8. Ibid., p. 186.
9. Fredric Jameson, *The Political Unconscious: Narrative as a Socially Symbolic Act* (Ithaca, N.Y.: Cornell University Press, 1981), p. 36.
10. *Reading Capital*, pp. 98–100.
11. Raymond Williams, *Keywords: A Vocabulary of Culture and Society* (New York: Oxford University Press, 1976), pp. 150–54.
12. Jacques Derrida, *Edmund Husserl's "The Origin of Geometry": An Introduction*, trans. with a preface by John P. Leavey, Jr. (Stony Brook, N.Y.: Nicolas Hays Ltd., 1978), pp. 48–51.
13. Ernst Robert Curtius, *European Literature and the Latin Middle Ages*, trans. Willard R. Trask (Princeton, N.J.: Princeton University Press, 1973), p. 54.
14. Ibid., pp. 51, 267.
15. Ibid., pp. 394–95, 396–97, 398.

16. Ibid., p. 397.

17. T. S. Eliot, *Christianity and Culture* [containing "The Idea of a Christian Society" and " Notes Toward the Definition of Culture"] (New York: Harcourt, Brace, Jovanovich, 1968), pp. 195–96, 197.

18. Matthew Arnold, *Culture and Anarchy*, ed. with an introduction by J. Dover Wilson (Cambridge: Cambridge University Press, 1978), pp. 70–71.

19. Herbert Marcuse, *Negations: Essays in Critical Theory*, trans. Jeremy J. Shapiro (Boston: Beacon Press, 1968), p. 95.

20. Quoted by Frank Kermode in *The Classic: Literary Images of Permanence and Change* (New York: Viking Press, 1975), p. 15.

21. Alexander Pope, "An Essay on Criticism," in *Critical Theory Since Plato*, ed. Hazard Adams (New York: Harcourt, Brace, Jovanovich, 1971), p. 279.

22. Ibid., p. 286.

23. Ibid., p. 280.

24. Horace, *Epistle to the Pisos*, in *Critical Theory Since Plato*, pp. 68–75, passim.

25. Sir Joshua Reynolds, "Discourse III," in *Critical Theory Since Plato*, pp. 354–59, passim.

26. Lodovico Castelvetro, from *The "Poetics" of Aristotle Translated and Annotated* in *Literary Criticism: Plato to Dryden*, ed. Allan H. Gilbert (Detroit, Mich.: Wayne State University Press, 1962), pp. 329–30.

27. Samuel Johnson, from "Preface to *Shakespeare*," in *Critical Theory Since Plato*, pp. 331, 333. W. K. Wimsatt and Cleanth Brooks, *Literary Criticism: A Short History* (New York: Alfred A. Knopf, 1962), p. 325.

28. Kenneth Burke, *A Grammar of Motives* (Berkeley and Los Angeles: University of California Press, 1969), pp. 118–19. See also *Permanence and Change: An Anatomy of Purpose* (Los Altos, Calif.: Hermes Publications, 1954), pp. 40–43.

29. *The Classic*, pp. 21, 31, 40, 72.

30. *Selections from the Prison Notebooks of Antonio Gramsci*, ed. and trans. Quintin Hoare and Geoffrey Nowell Smith (New York: International Publishers, 1971), p. 324.

Part Five

1. Kenneth Burke, *Permanence and Change: An Anatomy of Purpose* (Los Altos, Calif.: Hermes Publications, 1954), p. 88.

2. Kenneth Burke, *A Rhetoric of Motives* (Berkeley and Los Angeles: University of California Press, 1969), p. 172.

3. Ibid., p. xiii.

4. *Permanence and Change*, p. 212.

5. Ibid., p. 40.

6. *A Rhetoric of Motives*, pp. 23, 146.

7. Ibid., p. 22.

8. Ibid., pp. 27–31, passim.

9. Ibid., p. 60.

10. See Frank Lentricchia, "Reading Foucault (Punishment, Labor, Resistance)," *Raritan* (Spring 1982), 5–32; (Summer 1982), 41–70.

11. *A Rhetoric of Motives*, pp. 27–28.

12. Ibid., p. 30.

13. Ibid., p. 28.

14. Kenneth Burke, *The Philosophy of Literary Form: Studies in Symbolic Action* (Berkeley and Los Angeles: University of California Press, 1973), pp. 1, 3–6, 18–19, 25–27, 109.

15. Ibid., p. 26.

16. Jacques Derrida, "Freud and the Scene of Writing," in *Writing and Difference*, trans. with an introduction by Alan Bass (Chicago: University of Chicago Press, 1978), p. 226.

17. *The Philosophy of Literary Form*, p. 26.

18. Ibid., p. 26n.

19. Ibid., pp. 61, 191.

20. Ibid., p. 61.

21. Ibid., p. 64.

22. Ibid., p. 63.

23. Ibid., pp. 191–220 ("The Rhetoric of Hitler's 'Battle'"), esp. p. 200.

24. *A Rhetoric of Motives*, p. xiii.

25. *The Philosophy of Literary Form*, pp. 110–11.

26. *A Rhetoric of Motives*, p. 50.

27. Ibid., p. 25.